In Print!

In Print!

40 Cool Publishing Projects for Kids

Joe Rhatigan

LARK BOOKS

A DIVISION OF STERLING PUBLISHING CO., INC.
NEW YORK

*This book is dedicated to
Ms. Dopman, Mr. Mucciolo,
Mr. Haddad, and
Professor Cheney—
I wouldn't be the writer
I am today without them.*

Art Director
Celia Naranjo

Photographer
Steve Mann

Cover Designer
Barbara Zaretsky

Line Illustrations
Orrin Lundgren

Illustration Colorings
Celia Naranjo

Digital Photography Effects
Celia Naranjo & Shannon Yokeley

Assistant Editor
Rain Newcomb

Art Assistant
Shannon Yokeley

Editorial Assistance
Delores Gosnell

Art Intern
Lorelei Buckley

A NOTE ABOUT SUPPLIERS

Usually, the supplies you need for making the projects in Lark books can be found at your local craft supply store, discount mart, home improvement center, or retail shop relevant to the topic of the book. Occasionally, however, you may need to buy materials or tools from specialty suppliers. In order to provide you with the most up-to-date information, we have created a listing of suppliers on our website, which we update on a regular basis. Visit us at www.larkbooks.com, click on "Craft Supply Sources," and then click on the relevant topic. You will find numerous companies listed with their web address and/or mailing address and phone number.

10 9 8 7 6 5 4 3 2 1

Published by Lark Books, a division of
Sterling Publishing Co., Inc.
387 Park Avenue South, New York, N.Y. 10016

First Paperback Edition 2004
©2003, Lark Books

Distributed in Canada by Sterling Publishing
c/o Canadian Manda Group, One Atlantic Ave., Suite 105
Toronto, Ontario, Canada M6K 3E7

Distributed in the U.K. by
Guild of Master Craftsman Publications Ltd.
Castle Place, 166 High Street, Lewes, East Sussex, England
BN7 1XU
Tel: (+ 44) 1273 477374, Fax: (+ 44) 1273 478606, Email:
pubs@thegmcgroup.com, Web: www.gmcpublications.com

Distributed in Australia by Capricorn Link (Australia) Pty Ltd.
P.O. Box 704, Windsor, NSW 2756 Australia

If you have questions or comments about this book, please contact:
Lark Books
67 Broadway
Asheville, NC 28801
(828) 253-0467

Manufactured in China

ISBN: 1-57990-359-2 (hardcover) 1-57990-609-5 (paperback)

Contents

AMAZING WRITING SECRETS REVEALED HERE: page 8

You don't need superpowers to be a good writer. You also don't need to be born with a certain number of brain cells and IQ points. What you do need is a plan. Where can you find such a plan? Right here. Questions will be answered; fears will be allayed. Get ready to kick-start your life as a writer.

DESIGN DECISIONS: page 12

This book focuses on creative, fun, publishing projects that don't simply rely on white paper and pens. So, get out your paints, find some rubber stamps, stencils, and markers, and start designing. Even if you think you're not artistic, this chapter provides fun and simple tips (and tricks) for creating projects that not only read great, but look great as well.

THE PROJECTS: page 21

Getting your words in print doesn't simply mean magazines, books, and newspapers. The publishing projects included here show you unique and creative ways you can get your words out there yourself, whether in a book you can wear around your neck or one that fits in a tin can. Or how about publishing on a T-shirt, umbrella, stepping stones, a postcard the size of a small street sign? It's all here! Also included: activities for improving your skills as a writer, advice from young writers, and more.

GETTING PUBLISHED: page 106

Want a wider audience? Then it's time to pitch your writing to magazines, newspapers, and newsletters. And everything you need to know about preparing and submitting your manuscripts to real, live editors can be found right here.

COOL PLACES TO SEND YOUR WRITING: page 116

This is a selected list of magazines that accept submissions from young writers.

Hey You! Read This.

Thanks. Do you realize that by simply reading this introduction you're fulfilling my lifelong dream of being a writer? I can't remember a time when I didn't want to be one. In fact, the only thing I wanted to be more than a writer was a **published** writer. Now, here we are, just like I always imagined it. **Wow.**

What do you hope to accomplish as a writer? Do you want to see your name on the cover of a best-seller, or are you happy sharing your work with family and a few friends? Do you want your writing to make people think, laugh, or change their minds about something? For all these reasons and more, it's time to somehow get your words Out There.

A Self-Publishing Adventure
...with a Twist

Self publishing means that instead of relying on a book publisher, magazine, or newspaper, you publish your writing yourself. You can make photocopies of a bunch of poems and hand them out to friends, post an essay or novel on a web-site, or even write, print, and sell your own book. So, instead of simply being the author, you're also a designer, publicist, and publisher. You're in charge of how your writing looks and who gets to read it.

In Print not only explores and celebrates this creative and totally fun do-it-yourself publishing attitude, but also takes it a step further. (Here's the twist!) Sure, your poem looks great on paper, but instead of making a paper airplane out of it or filing it away in the deep, dark recesses of your desk, how about crafting a fun project with your poem on it? You could rubber stamp the poem onto an umbrella along with some friendly hand-painted frogs. Or, mail it to a friend on a postcard the size of a small street sign. You could even include it in an incredibly awesome cardboard book that's held together with nuts and bolts. These are just a few examples of the projects you'll find in this book—fun, imaginative projects that combine words and crafts to give your creative writing the attention it deserves.

Do you need to be a great writer to do these projects? No. In fact, these crafts are a great way to get yourself started on a writing adventure. Do you need to be a budding artist? Absolutely not. If you can use a pair of scissors and know how to take the cap off a marker, you're set.

Now, before you say, "Hey, that's not really publishing," think about this: most of the time, we put words on paper knowing or hoping somebody else will read them. When someone comes into your room and sees the totally cool, can't-take-my-eyes-off-it poetry curtain in your doorway, they will read it. And guess what? You've just made a connection with a reader. You're officially in print!

WHAT ELSE?

Hey, we're not done yet. There's more.

☞ Chapter 1 explores how to brainstorm writing ideas, take those ideas through the writing process, and then prepare the writing for publication.

☞ Chapter 2 includes simple tips on designing your publishing crafts.

☞ In Chapter 3, besides the projects, there are tons of fun activities for making your writing better and finding ideas to write about. The writing used for each project appears on decorative paper along with the project. By the way, the poems, stories, and articles used were written by young writers such as yourself.

☞ Finally, if you want more than a few friends to read your writing, Chapter 4 is an easy-to-use guide to what you need to know when it comes to submitting your work to magazines, newspapers, and newsletters, including a selected list of magazines that accept submissions from young writers.

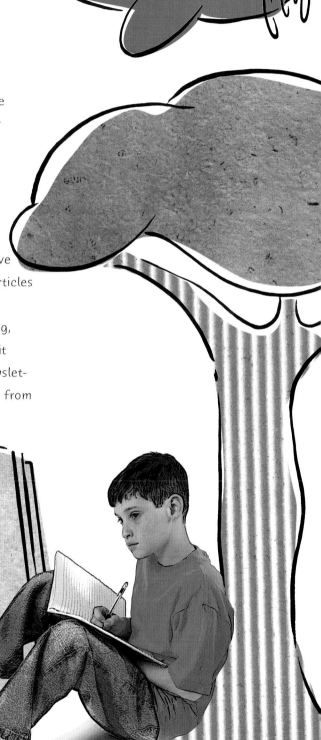

I wrote this book primarily to celebrate words. They're indispensable little tools that have the incredible power to touch people. They can change the world. Seeing your words in handmade books, gifts, and other unique projects can be an exhilarating experience, and lead to other wonderful creative journeys in the future. My hope for you? That the writing adventure you've undertaken lasts a lifetime... and then some. Have fun!

1

Amazing Writing Secrets Revealed Here!

Before you publish your writing, you need to write it. And if you're just starting out, you may need a little help. Look no further, you've come to the right place. And even if you've been writing for a bit, this chapter will still be helpful. I've included information on getting started, finding a good place to create, brainstorming, editing, and more. There are lots of books on how to write, and I won't even pretend to add everything I know or should know. I've simply provided simple things to do to get started. You'll figure out the rest, I promise. Speaking of promises, I'm supposed to reveal amazing writing secrets. So, before we go any further, here they are:

SECRET #1

The only thing you have to do in order to be a writer is write. Sound too simple to be true? Well, it's true. That doesn't mean you're a published writer or even a good writer, it just means that you enjoy playing with words and expressing ideas on paper or a computer screen. And although there are a ton of perfectly fine "how to write" books out there, they can't force your fingers to grab a pen and put words on a piece of paper. Only you can do that. That leads to the second secret.

SECRET #2

There is no one right way to write. Everyone does it differently, and in order to grow and mature as a writer, you'll sooner or later have to come up with your own habits, rituals, and techniques. Use how-to information to get started, but never be afraid to do something differently. In other words, if something doesn't work for you, try something else.

SECRET #3

You never have to pretend to be a writer. What's so great about writing is that, unlike a lot of other professions, you can do it right now. You can even make money right now or at least get the satisfaction of seeing your name in print. Remember when you were younger and wanted to be a doctor or firefighter, and you played and pretended. With writing, you never have to pretend, though you'll practice the art for the rest of your life. You'll get better if you keep doing it.

THE WRITING PROCESS

Although there's no one right way to write (see secret #2), there are tons of tried and true techniques you can try if you're having problems with certain aspects of your writing. Most teachers and writing books call how writers get down to the business of actually writing something **the writing process**, which includes how to find ideas, how to get them on paper, and how to edit and polish them. The next couple of pages will focus on original and fun ways to help you do all that and more.

I Want to Write, but I Have Nothing to Write About!

I hate when that happens. It's pretty frustrating, and it can ruin your whole writing mood. So, what to do, what to do? I like to think about all the possible solutions to this problem as tricking the brain into seeing, hearing, smelling, tasting, feeling (EXPERIENCING) the totally word-worthy world around us. Sometimes the best writing topics are right there in front of our faces, and we don't even notice them. One of my better tricks is to **take a hot shower**. Really. I can't explain why, but it works. If you're stumped, take a shower, and bring along some bathtub crayons (since bringing your notebook with you isn't the brightest idea). Once

you're in the shower, try to avoid thinking about your homework and other chores you have to do. Relax, and see what happens. Keep the crayons nearby.

Here are some other tips:

✎ One of the few important pieces of equipment necessary for a writer is a notebook. Get one—any kind you're comfortable with. Write down all your ideas in it, and bring it with you everywhere. When you notice something or an idea hits you, write down a line or two to remind you of your thought, and go about your business. The next time you sit down to write, it'll be there. Your observation could be a smell, a sound, a flashback (just like the movies), something funny a friend said, space aliens, anything. Even if you don't know what you'll end up doing with these observations at least they'll be there,

and you won't be able to say, "Gee, I had a great idea but I forgot it."

✎ Write on the bus or some other unusual place, such as a cafeteria or restaurant. You may hear interesting bits of conversation, notice an intriguing person you wish you knew more about, or the change of scenery may jostle your brain enough to get some ideas flowing.

✎ Keep your notebook by your bed, and just before you fall asleep, think about your day and different things you can write about. Also, write down your dreams as soon as you wake up in the morning.

✏ Read. A lot. Use what you read as inspiration. Try to write in the style of your favorite poets and writers. Just read. A writer who doesn't read is like a cook who doesn't eat.

✏ Get your hands on some pictures of art. (Even better, go to a museum.) Imagine the lives of the people in the paintings or simply describe what you see.

✏ Write not only about your life, but tape record your grandparents' life stories and write about them.

When trying to think of something to write about, try to keep this in mind: your writing doesn't have to be on a topic nobody has ever written about before. There's nothing wrong with writing about apples or clouds. Don't limit yourself; you won't know if a topic is worth writing about until you try. And, by simply being open to experience and life, you may soon find yourself deluged with ideas.

Find a Place to Write

Figure out your favorite places to write. I love writing in the kitchen after dinner. Sometimes the whir of the dishwasher drowns out any other family noises. It's perfect for me. Your room may be a good place to start, but experiment. Do you like complete silence, or does some noise help you focus? Do you like to sit, lie, stand on your head? By the way, I don't know of too many successful writers who can write in front of the television.

Also, a word or two on another piece of essential equipment: a favorite pen. Get a pen that screams, "REALLY GREAT WORDS COME OUT OF ME!"

What else you may need:

✏ An awesome unabridged dictionary (one with all the words in it)

✏ A usage book that gives you lots of hints on common writing mistakes

✏ A thesaurus? If you've got one, that's fine. Just don't overuse it. A propensity for utilizing impressively sized utterances appears cumbersome and maladroit. (See what I mean?) It's not the size and complexity of the words you choose, but how you use the words you know that makes you a writer.

Brainstorming

After finding an idea, it's time to brainstorm, or gather all your information on the subject that's in your head. Sometimes finding an idea leads right into brainstorming, which leads right into a first draft. That's cool. Don't mess with the flow, just keep rolling along. Here are a few brainstorming techniques. (Don't be afraid to develop your own.):

✏ Write down everything you already know about the subject or everything you know you want in the story. This doesn't have to be pretty writing. Just slap it on the page or screen. Then, start asking questions (Who? What? Where? When? Why? How?), and write the questions down. Then, answer the questions as completely as you can.

✏ Create lots of lists.

✏ Freewrite: start writing and don't stop. Set a timer and don't let the pen leave the page for that time period.

✏ At some point during the brainstorming, you may want to start thinking of an outline. Works for some. For others, it doesn't. I don't use outlines for poems, though for this book I revised my outline 13 times over the course of a month. And the funny thing is, as I wrote it, the outline changed again anyway.

The Curse of the First Draft

Once your brainstorming feels complete, you'll most likely set yourself up in front of your computer or settle into your favorite writing spot with your favorite pen and notebook, along with all the great brainstorming ideas you generated and...start writing your first draft.

Right off the bat, you may need to adjust your attitude about this first draft. The first draft is the mound of clay that will eventually become a piece of sculpture. It is not the sculpture itself. So:

✏ Don't worry about spelling, punctuation, or even whether or not you're making perfect sense—just get the words on the page.

✏ Worrying too much about making it perfect the first time out may cause you to suffer from the **Blank Page Syndrome**. That's when you stare at the blank page, not knowing what to do next, until you give up, and turn on the TV.

✏ If you can't think of a first sentence or line, write the second sentence first. If you can't think of an introduction, write the conclusion first.

Like many beginning writers, you may fall under the **CURSE OF THE FIRST DRAFT.** That's when you write your first draft and fall instantly in love with it. You never want to look at it again.

It's perfect...done. The spell isn't usually broken until someone else reads it and goes "huh?!" Almost 100 percent of the time, your first draft won't look too much like your final draft. The first draft is for your eyes only. It's full of ugly spelling mistakes, confusing sentences, and nightmarish construction. Why? Because the first draft is for getting the ideas on paper. And, If you're too worried about the spelling and punctuation at this point, the ideas won't make it onto

the paper. In some cases you may not even get beyond the first sentence. If you fall in love with the first draft, you'll never be able to revise it. Remember the mound of clay—you're just starting to get your hands dirty.

Getting Unstuck

If you get stuck while writing, stop for a moment and read what you wrote. That sometimes works in getting unstuck. Also, at some point during this first draft you're going to realize that you either want to keep writing, or you don't like the topic at all. Just remember that there's no reason to keep writing about something that's boring you to tears. This isn't homework.

So, imagine yourself sitting in your favorite writing spot working away at a first draft. You don't care about punctuation. You're not worried about spelling. Heck, you can barely even read it. But you're getting it on paper. It's a great way to start.

Now What?

Sure you wrote your first draft, but did you read it? Keep a pen in your hand and simply circle words, sentences, paragraphs...whatever doesn't sound right. But don't stop to fix things, yet. Just read it. When you've finished reading, read it again...out loud. Maybe pretend someone else is listening. What does this imaginary person think of it? Or, pretend you're not the author.

Revise It

Revision...re vision...re look...see again. Get it?

Revising your writing is probably the most important part of the writing process. Why? Because you're not done yet. Your mound of clay hasn't taken shape. It doesn't look like much. Revision is a lot more radical than simply checking your spelling. It can mean cutting whole sections and adding new ones, rewriting, creating new characters, writing new stanzas, and basically, getting the words right so they mean exactly what you want them to mean in an interesting manner that readers will enjoy. This doesn't happen magically. It takes time, patience, creativity, and oftentimes, some major surgery. Check out these tips:

✏ After your first draft, take a break and let it breathe. Take a day or two, or, if necessary, a week. Work on something else.

✏ Get rid of as many forms of "to be" (is, am, are, was, were). Each time you do, you end up with a stronger sentence. Here's an example: **Boring & too long**
1) My bike is beautiful and fast. It is the envy of the neighborhood. **Revised & strOnger**
2) The neighbors envy my fast and beautiful bike.

Not only is the sentence stronger, but it took

two sentences and shortened them into one. Cutting words is the best kind of revising you can do.

✏ Look at your possibilities. Would your piece be better without your introduction? Read it without it. You'll be surprised how many times this is

true. Do all your paragraphs make sense? Does your poem read better when read from the end to the beginning? (Hey, you never know.)
✏ When you're getting pretty happy with your piece, read it to somebody, or let someone else read it. Choose this person carefully. Don't pick your best friend who thinks everything is "totally awesome, man." And sorry, but if your mom thinks that even your list of things to do is a masterpiece, don't use her to help you revise. Many teachers will love to help you out. Other writers your own age can also be a help.

Listen to this person who's critiquing your work, and make changes in the places where you agree. But also look at the places where you don't agree. Are you being stubborn, or is your reader off base there?
✏ With each draft, start looking at spelling, usage, and punctuation.
✏ Keep revising until...until.... When do you stop? That's a good question. When the piece looks the way you want it to, and every word has a purpose and it's where you want it to be, you're done. Though it's often difficult to know when you're finished revising, you'll get better at knowing the more you do it.

Proofread

Time for some proofreading. At this point, you probably won't be making any more drastic changes to your piece. You're now in the fine-

tuning stage where you'll make sure your spelling, punctuation, and usage are correct. And just because you have trouble keeping things like "there," "their," and "they're" straight doesn't mean you don't have what it takes to be a good writer.

First of all, find a good usage book. It's a valuable reference book for this stage of the writing process. It will clear up ambiguous words and punctuation decisions.

Second, begin a proofreading list in the back of your notebook. Every time you look up something in the usage book, such as when to use a semi-colon, write the rule in the back of the notebook. Keep track of them, and soon you'll be able to refer to your notebook to fix mistakes you tend to make all the time. And after you know you've got one of the rules down pat, highlight it.

Finally, after all that, get someone else to read it over for you. I actually get to hire a proofreader to read this book before it gets published. You'll have to find someone you trust, such as a teacher, parent, or older sibling. Buy them a candy bar as payment. Never underestimate the power of snacks.

The Final Questions

Though there are no certainties when it comes to taste (nobody can promise you that everyone will like your writing), there are ways of making sure your early publishing

career avoids much of the awful stuff. This is what it comes down to: whether you're creating a publishing project or trying to get published in a favorite magazine, your writing should say exactly what you want it to say, and be clear, concise, and free of spelling and punctuation errors. How you get your writing to that point is up to you. Like I said, every writer does it differently.

But how do you know you're ready to publish? Ask yourself these questions:
✏ Is my piece worth the reader's time?
✏ Have I written something worthwhile, fun, and/or useful for readers?
✏ Is this something I really want to share with people? Is it something that's harshly critical of someone whom I don't really want to hurt? Is it something best left in my journal?

If you decide to read the writing books out there, pick the strategies that work for you. Keep thinking about what works and doesn't work. Develop a process that fits your style. Hone it. Experiment with different strategies.

Now, it's time to

turn the

page....

Design Decisions

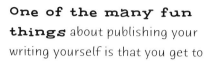

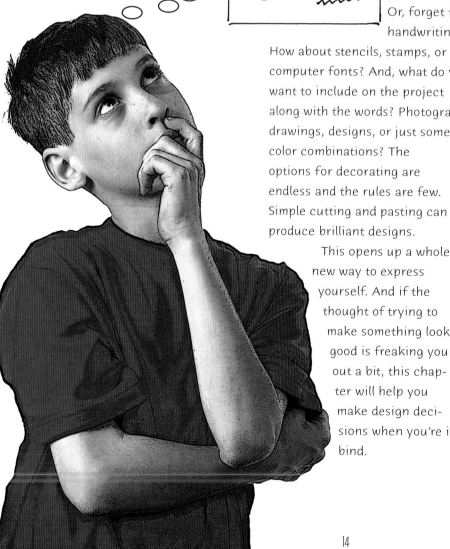

One of the many fun things about publishing your writing yourself is that you get to decide how your words appear on the project. Will you try some calligraphy, or will simple handwriting be good enough? Or, forget the handwriting. How about stencils, stamps, or computer fonts? And, what do you want to include on the project along with the words? Photographs, drawings, designs, or just some fun color combinations? The options for decorating are endless and the rules are few. Simple cutting and pasting can produce brilliant designs.

This opens up a whole new way to express yourself. And if the thought of trying to make something look good is freaking you out a bit, this chapter will help you make design decisions when you're in a bind.

CRAFT TECHNIQUES TO ADD SPARK TO YOUR DESIGNS

Here are a few fun ways you can create your words and images. You don't need to be an artist to do them; in fact, even if you can barely draw stick figures, you can do these and look like a pro.

Stenciling

Stenciling is simply painting through a hole (or pattern of holes) cut in a piece of material that you've taped against the surface of your project. All you need is a stencil (the pattern), paint, tape, and a foam brush or can of spray paint. You can find all sorts of designs and letter sizes and shapes

at craft stores. You can also design your own stencils and cut them out of thin cardboard.

Letters

Choose different fonts or letter styles so you'll have ones that suit various moods and purposes. You can also use letter stencils for the basic letter shape, then decorate the letters to fit your own taste. Find stencils that are a good size for the project you're working on. Paint them, or outline with a good pen—then you can color them in.

Basic steps for stenciling:

1. Use tape to attach the stencils in place. If you're creating a border or another design that must be perfectly placed, use a carpenter's level to draw a line you can use to make sure the edges of your stencils are positioned correctly.

2. Dab on paint to fill the stencil's cutout area with a foam brush. Don't drag your brush over the stencil; you risk driving paint under the stencil and outside the design's border.

3. Gently remove the stencils, being careful not to smudge the painted design as you do.

Stamps

Create awesome designs with store-bought or homemade stamps. Printing with stamps is a fun way to add images to your projects, and it's easy to make your own. You can stamp words, images, and fun designs anywhere you see fit to do so. You can also use leaves, stones, tree bark, and vegetable or fruit slices. You simply press your stamp on an ink pad or dip it in acrylic paint, test it on a piece of scrap paper, and start stamping. You can also use markers to ink the stamps. To make your own stamps, cut designs out of sponges with sharp scissors or cut out cardboard shapes and glue them to rectangular pieces of cardboard.

Painting

Draw, sponge, stencil, and splatter paint on your projects as you want. Most of the projects call for acrylic craft paints. These paints are good because they dry quickly and can be used to cover almost any surface.

You can use them straight from the tubes, though using a palette or plastic plate can be helpful when mixing and experimenting with colors. Use sandpaper to rough up metal surfaces so that paint will stick to them better, and mix in a little glue with your paint for plastic objects. Glow-in-the-dark paints and three-dimensional (3-D) paints are great for special effects. If you use spray paint, make sure you work outdoors so you get plenty of fresh air. Protect your painted projects by coating the surface with a water-based sealer, acrylic spray enamel, or a couple of coats of decoupage glue.

Collage

You've been making collages since the day your parents finally trusted you with a pair of scissors, and they're still fun today. Collect images and mementos that relate to your writing, arrange them in a fun and interesting way, and, when you're happy with how it looks, break out the glue. So, rip, tear, scrounge from magazines, old books, and digital images, and improvise away.

Decoupage

Decoupage is what you do when you make a collage or design by cutting and pasting layers of paper to cover the surface of an object. To make your own decoupage glue, mix four parts white craft glue to one part water in a glass jar. Cover it with a lid so it'll be ready to use for your collages and decoupage projects. This watered-down glue mixture also makes a great protective coating over paper and fabric projects.

LAYOUT BASICS

Words and images often go hand in hand. Would you even consider reading a magazine that had no pictures? And what about all those picture books you read as a little kid? If you worked at a magazine as a writer, you'd have little say in these decisions. Graphic designers are the ones who'd take your words and decide how they will look on the page. This overall design is called a *layout*. Here, you get to make these important decisions yourself. The next few pages discuss easy tips you can use to combine words and images in appealing and artistic ways.

Sketches

It's a good idea to sketch out your ideas first. It may not be exactly what you'll do in the end, but it will serve as a map to help get you started. It's a good idea to keep your sketches in a notebook. Some of your ideas might not work for one project, but you may find it's perfect for another project later on.

Composition

Composition is the way you place words and images on a page or project. When you lay out a page with a pleasing composition, you can control the order in which the page is read. A good composition makes a page easy to read and understand. Compositions are read from left to right and up to down, just like read-

> Yesterday
> Alex Cole-Weiss
>
> Yesterday
> I fell to the floor—
> a broken vase with
> flowers strewn among
> the wet glass.
> What do you do when you're
> broken?
> Each piece of blue glass
> seems to not fit back together.
> But did they ever?
> The only thing that stays
> the same is change.
> Every fall is change.
> And if you wish not to break,
> replace the flowers.

Figure 1

Figure 2

Figure 3

ing a book. For example, in figure 1, the elements make a big X. You automatically read the top left first, see the picture, and read the bottom right last. With this composition, all the elements relate to each other but look like they're part of the same unit. Other common layout patterns are S and O shapes (figures 2 and 3).

Grids

Along with good composition, you also want your words and elements to line up on a *grid*. Grids are invisible lines formed by common edges of the word blocks and images on your page. Like a composition, it helps your reader know where to look next. When you lay out a page without a grid, your eye jumps to all the different edges, and your page can look too busy and messy. A grid helps the reader understand the flow of how to read your page. Many times it helps to sketch your ideas on grid paper; this way you know they'll line up. Figure 4 looks

a little messy. Notice that by simply shifting some of the words and pictures to line up to a grid, the page is now neater and easier to read (figure 5).

Typography

There are many different typefaces. Each one can be used to help a layout look different. Think about what the project is about and how you want the reader to feel.

The most important thing to remember when you pick a typeface is to make sure it's easy to read. There are some fun fonts out there that seem to have great shapes or curves. These are easier to read if you use them very sparingly. If there

Too many fancy letters can make it hard to read your writing.

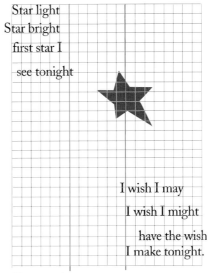

Figure 4

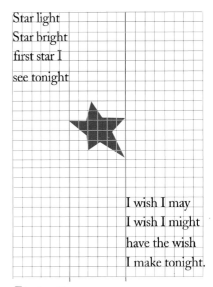

Figure 5

are too many fancy letters, it's hard to read the words. Don't use more than a couple of typefaces in a project. Too many different typefaces can be confusing.

Negative and Positive Space

You don't have to fill up all the blank spots in a page or project. Sometimes when blank space surrounds an image or your writing, it

Figure 6

highlights them. The space covered by images and words is called *positive space*, and areas that are blank are *negative* or *white space* (figure 6). White space can also be considered an element in your composition. The most important place for white space is on the edges of your page or project. It helps frame your layout (figure 7).

Star light
Star bright
first star I
see tonight
I wish I may
I wish I might
have the wish
I make tonight.

Figure 7

Color Theory

It's not necessary to use a lot of color in your projects. Sometimes a small dot of color can have more

Figure 8

impact. If you use too many strong colors together, it might make it hard to read the words or images (figure 8). Pay attention to books and pictures you like and what colors are used together. You can use these same color combinations when you make your projects.

OTHER IMPORTANT STUFF

Avoid future headaches by doing a little preparation before jumping into the projects in this book. You'll save time and make fewer mistakes by gathering all the tools you need, setting up your work space, and figuring out how to clean up before you cut that first piece of cardboard or start squeezing the glue.

Work Space

Successful artists and crafters have studios, so set up a space in your room or in your house where you can work on your projects. Choose an area that has a table or large floor space to work on, and protect the surface by covering it with newspapers or a large sheet. You'll likely need a window for ventilation and an electrical outlet nearby. If you have pets or younger siblings, be certain they won't be able to get into your crafting tools and materials when you're not watching. The ideal work space allows you to leave your projects and materials overnight without anyone or anything getting into them.

Paper

Paper isn't just the white stuff you print your homework out on. There are tons of different kinds of paper in all sorts of different colors, designs, sizes, shapes, and textures. Explore your local art supply, craft, or even office supply stores for fun paper to use for your projects. Here is the lowdown on the types of paper used in many of the projects in this book:

Printer or photocopy paper: This is the stuff you print your homework out on, though you can find it in a rainbow of colors. It's also known as text-weight paper.

Card stock or cover-weight paper: This paper is bulkier than printer paper. It feels a little like the lightweight cardboard you have to take out of your brand new shirts before you can wear them.

Decorative paper: This is any type of paper that has a design on it. It could be tissue paper, wrapping paper, wallpaper, or any other cool paper you find.

Handmade style: This paper looks like it's handmade, so it usually has rough edges and may have leaves, newspaper, or other fun stuff embedded in it.

Construction paper: If you don't know what this is, sue your kindergarten teacher.

Mat board and poster board: Available at art supply stores, these types of paper are good for book covers.

Foam board: Though technically not paper, this thick board is stiff and needs to be cut with a craft knife.

Folding, Cutting, and Gluing Paper

Paper and board can be cut with scissors or with a craft knife. Bone folders are made specifically for scoring paper to make neat folds, and are available at art supply stores. If you don't want to buy one, you can use a butter knife instead.

To fold paper, use a metal ruler as a guide, and mark a line where you want the paper to fold with a few light pencil dots. Score the line by running the pointed end of a bone folder or butter knife along it, using the metal ruler as a guide once again (figure 9). This breaks the top fibers in the paper, making it easier to fold. Fold the page where you just scored it, and rub

Figure 9

Figure 10

the wide end of the bone cutter (or the flat side of the butter knife) along the crease in order to make it crisp (figure 10).

When cutting paper, use scissors or a craft knife. If you want to use a craft knife, make sure you get an adult to help you out at first. Place a cutting board or piece of cardboard on your work surface. Place the paper on top of the cutting surface, and use the ruler as a guide. Hold the craft knife firmly in one hand and press the tip of the knife into the paper. Slowly drag the knife toward you to make a cut (figure 11). Never leave craft knives out where pets or young kids might find them.

Figure 11

When gluing, you want the glue to evenly coat the entire surface of the paper you're sticking to the project, edges and all. Do this all on your work surface or use a cutting mat (available at, you guessed it, craft and art supply stores).

Cool Handwriting

If you've got it, consider yourself lucky. If your handwriting looks like someone (or something) just attacked the page with the pen, don't give up hope. Experiment with different pens, gel pens, metallic pens, feathers, twigs, pencils, colored pencils, crayons (gotta love crayons), paints, watercolors, chalk, and more. Perhaps the right writing instrument is all you need. Practice some of the handwriting samples on this page with the different types of pens. You may be surprised by the results. If, however, your handwriting simply stinks, and there's nothing to be done about it, don't pack it in just yet. Let your computer come to the rescue. Most word-processing programs come chock full of wonderful fonts. Experiment to your heart's content.

It Had to be Said...

Write what you like best.
—Devon Dickerson, age 9

once upon a time

once upon a time

once upon a time

ONCE UPON A TIME

Once Upon a time

★ Once Upon A Time ★

Once Upon A Time

once upon a time

The Projects

Along with the wonderful projects (if I do say so myself) in this chapter, there are also these features:

ACTIVITIES: These either help with your writing, give you ways to make your writing stronger, or simply show you how to have fun with your writing.

BRAINSTORMING: Every now and then, a project will be followed by an activity that may help you the next time you need something to write about.

YOUNG WRITERS AT WORK: Young writers answer questions about how they write.

And enjoy the work from real young writers that we've included with the projects.

BEFORE YOU START

✏ When transferring your words onto a project, beware of weird errors that suddenly show up. Misspellings and transposed or dropped letters tend to occur when transferring, so keep a printout of a thoroughly proofread manuscript on your worktable as you do each project. Refer to it often, and read what you've done as you work.

✏ Either choose a project that looks right for the writing you're interested in seeing in print, or use the projects as sparks for writing ideas.

✏ Make sure the project and your writing are a good fit. You may not want to publish your 30,000-word novel on a T-shirt.

✏ Your projects will not look exactly the same as the ones in this book. Your images and words will not be the same, and nobody has the same tastes in everything. Experiment and have a great time.

Beware misspellings and transposed or missing letters!

GARGE SALE TODAY!

BOOKS

MEMORY FRAME

The next time you're inspired to write about somebody you care for, write your words on a frame to surround a favorite photograph of that special person.

ON GRANDFATHER'S LAP I LEARNED THUNDER WAS THE ANGELS BOWLING AND WHEN HUNGRY, THEY PICKED AT THE COTTON CANDY SKY.

WHAT YOU NEED

- Wooden picture frame with wide borders
- Acrylic paints in iridescent fuchsia and lavender (or any two colors that go well together)
- Paintbrush or foam brush
- Plastic wrap
- Scrap paper
- Scissors
- Short poem
- Ruler and pencil
- Alphabet rubber stamp set
- Black permanent ink pad
- Permanent black marker
- Photograph

WHAT YOU DO

1. Paint the frame with the fuchsia paint. It may take more than one coat to completely cover the wood. Just make sure to let each coat dry before putting on the next.

2. Crumple a piece of plastic wrap into a loose ball. Apply a thin coat of the lavender paint to the frame, then dab at it with the plastic wrap. This will remove some of the lavender paint and create an interesting shaded finish. Work fast, in sections, for this step since the paint dries quickly.

3. After the paint is dry, plan the placement of your poem carefully. It may help to cut a piece of scrap paper to the same size as the frame, and practice on it before stamping the actual frame.

4. If you like, use the ruler and pencil to draw light lines on the frame to guide you while stamping the letters. However, don't worry about lining everything up perfectly.

5. To stamp the frame, ink each letter by tapping it on the ink pad, then pressing the stamp firmly and evenly on the frame. Don't rock the stamp back and forth—this can smear the letters.

6. Add punctuation with a permanent marker, and insert the photo you want in the frame.

On Grandfather's Lap
K. Lee Evans

I learned thunder
was the angels bowling.
And when hungry,
they picked at
the cotton candy sky.

BRAINSTORMING

Look through family photo albums for old photographs of your grandparents or other ancestors. Choose one photo that particularly intrigues you. If you choose a black and white photograph, even better. Write a poem or story about what you think is happening in the photo. Ask yourself questions about what you think is going on. What are the people in the photo thinking about? Who's taking the picture? What's the occasion? You can ask questions of living relatives to fill in the missing information, or simply imagine the answers. Where are they? Why are they taking the picture right there, right then? Stamp your poem or a selection of the story onto a frame, and put the picture in the frame.

SIGNATURE EDITION BOUND BOOK

This simple-to-make book is sewn together with what's known as a **butterfly** or **pamphlet** stitch. The book shown here measures $4\frac{1}{2}$ x $5\frac{3}{4}$ inches (11.4 x 14.6 cm), though you can create all sorts of different-sized books.

WHAT YOU NEED

- 2 pieces of black text-weight paper, 8½ x 11 inches (21.6 x 27.9 cm)
- Ruler and pencil
- Scissors
- 1 piece of card stock, 5¾ x 9 inches (14.6 x 22.9 cm)
- Gift wrap, cut slightly larger than the card stock
- Glue stick
- Gold paint pen (optional)
- Needle
- Waxed linen* or dental floss
- Beads (optional)
- Your writing
- Gel pens and other design materials

*Available at bead shops and craft stores

It Had to be Said...

Anything can be an inspiration, whether it's a word or an everyday object; everything has a hidden piece of art in it. It's simply up to you to find it.

-Chelsea Smith, age 13

WHAT YOU DO

1. Cut each piece of the text-weight paper in half to create four pieces measuring 5½ x 8½ inches (14 x 21.6 cm).

2. One at a time, fold each of the pages carefully in half. Each folded page will now be 4¼ x 5½ inches (10.8 x 14 cm).

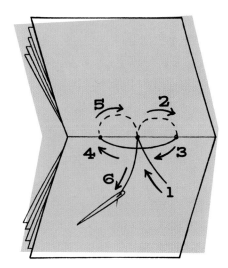

3. After folding, stack the pages together, and set them aside.

4. Glue the wrapping paper to the card stock. Trim away the extra paper. Color the edges with the gold paint pen if you want.

5. Fold the card stock in half. This is now the cover of your book.

6. Place the folded pages inside the cover, centering them in the fold.

7. Using the needle, carefully make three holes at the fold, piercing through all four folded papers and the cover. Space the holes evenly, making one at the center of the fold and the others on either side of the first, about 1½ inches (3.8 cm) away (figure 1).

8. Thread the needle with a piece of waxed linen or dental floss about 18 inches (45.7 cm) long.

9. From the outside, bring the needle into the center of the book through the middle hole. Take the needle back out at the top hole. Come back to the inside at the bottom hole. Finally, go out again at the center hole (see illustration). Unthread the needle and set it aside.

10. Turn the book over and look at the outside. You'll see the thread running along the spine from the top to bottom holes, and two tails of thread hanging from the center hole. Arrange the tails so that there is one on each side of the long stitch running along the side. Then, tie a knot. If you want, thread beads onto each tail, and tie knots at the ends to secure them before trimming the tails.

11. Write or glue your story or poems in the book. Decorate using gel pens or other items.

WHAT'S A SIGNATURE ANYWAY?

A signature is simply a stack of pages bound together in a book. A signature for books usually has 8, 16 or 32 pages. All the pages of a book are bound together in signatures so that the book doesn't bulge out. (Try folding a big stack of paper in half.) Signatures also make it easier to sew the pages together. See if you can figure out how many signatures this book has, and how many pages are in each signature.

Here are the names of other parts of a book:

Front and Back Covers: serve to protect the pages inside and keep the book closed

Spine: fastens the signatures together. When you place a book on a shelf, it's the spine that you see.

Spread: Anytime you have two facing pages

Gutter: the blank space in the middle of a spread (where the pages are folded).

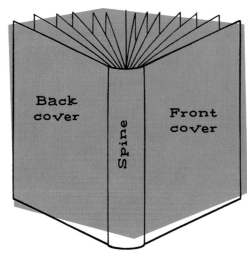

Back cover

Spine

Front cover

Margins: create breathing room for the words. Margins and gutter form a "frame" around the text.

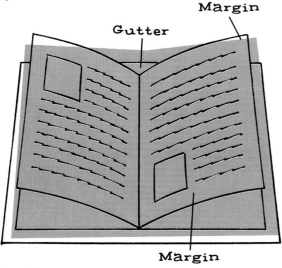

Margin

Gutter

Margin

Where do you find ideas for your writing?

I get ideas from everything.
—Adam Rush, age 12

My writing is influenced by nature and major happenings in the world.
—Hannah Currie, age 12

My ideas come from my life experiences, dreams, as well as books, plays, songs, and people I encounter. You can write about anything, the trick is to not be bound to your original topic. Ideas can be extracted from the edges of things you write and turned into works of their own.
—Caitlen Wood, age 13

I find ideas for writing by taking mental notes of the characteristics of the people I know and putting them into characters.
—Ty deVries, age 11

THE INCREDIBLE, SHRINKABLE CHARM BRACELET POEM

Shrinkable plastic sheets are available at craft, hobby, and toy stores. Simply write your poem on one plastic sheet, cut out the words in fun shapes, stick them in the oven, and voilà, your shapes are about one-third smaller and ready to be admired.

WHAT YOU DO

1. Decide how many charms you'll need for your poem. Design your shapes. Avoid creating long, thin shapes and shapes with sharp corners. These will tend to catch on things or break. Draw or trace the shapes you've decided to use on a sheet of paper.

2. Write the words of the poem in the shapes you just drew. Use a pencil so you can erase mistakes.

3. Place the shrinkable plastic sheet over the piece of paper. Use the markers to trace the words and the outline of the shapes. Also, add fun designs if you want.

4. Cut out the shapes with the scissors. Make sure to cut just inside the outlines, so when the plastic shrinks you don't end up with bits of ink from the outlines.

5. Use the hole punch to make a hole in each charm. Don't make the hole until you've decided how you want the charms to hang on the bracelet. Also, don't punch holes too close to the outer edges, or you'll create weak spots in the charms.

6. Place the charms on the cookie sheet, and follow the shrinkable plastic manufacturer's instructions for heating them. Take them out of

WHAT YOU NEED

- ✎ Paper and pencil
- ✎ Ruler
- ✎ Your poem
- ✎ Sheet of opaque, shrinkable plastic
- ✎ Permanent markers in black and red (or colors to complement the beads)
- ✎ Scissors
- ✎ Hole punch
- ✎ Cookie sheet
- ✎ Use of an oven
- ✎ Oven mitts
- ✎ Jump rings*
- ✎ Round-tip pliers
- ✎ Bracelet-sized memory wire**
- ✎ Wire cutters
- ✎ Beads (with holes big enough to string on the wire)

*Available at craft and bead stores
**This is coiled wire used to make necklaces, bracelets, and rings. You can find it at craft and bead stores.

Success Story

Jane Yolen wrote many of her homework assignments in verse. She got an A+ on her final paper in American History—and everything in it rhymed! She also wrote a musical for her class in first grade. Everybody was a different vegetable, and they all ended up in a big salad! So far, she has published well over 200 books for adults and kids of all ages.

the oven when they're done, and let them cool.

7. Use the round-tip pliers to work open the jump rings for the charms. Peel the charms off the cookie sheet, and place the rings in the holes in the charms and close them. Set the charms aside.

8. Use the wire cutters to cut the memory wire to the length you'd like. Two to three loops usually work well.

9. With the round-tip pliers, bend one of the ends of the wire into a small loop so the beads and charms won't fall off (figure 1).

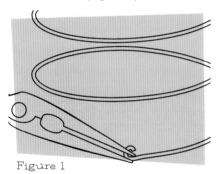

Figure 1

10. String the beads and charms onto the wire in any pattern you like. Make sure your charms are in order so you can read them. You may find placing smaller beads on each side of where a charm is located will allow the charm to move more freely.

11. When figuring where to place the charms, consider how they're spaced with the ones on the other loops so you don't end up with two charms overlapping each other a loop apart (figure 2).

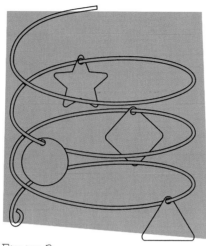

Figure 2

12. When finished beading, use the round-tip pliers to make a loop to finish the bracelet.

Diana
Brianna Huskey

There is one person
on this planet
who is greater
than the Stars,
sweeter than the Sun.
Her name is Diana,
and she is the Moon.

BRAINSTORMING

Sure you can write a poem on shrinkable plastic sheets, but what about a mini short story? Simply write a short story of yours on rectangular pieces of shrinkable plastic (the size is up to you), design the margins if you want, punch holes in the top left-hand corner of each sheet, and bake. String your story tablets on a piece of ribbon or string. Turn it into a necklace. If you make the tablets really small, get a magnifying glass so friends can read it. You can even buy shrinkable plastic computer paper now, which makes creating miniature publishing ventures even easier.

What else can you do?

☛ Send miniature letters to friends.

☛ Collect and trade shrinkable plastic friendship bracelet poems.

☛ Create poetry or personal statement pins.

☛ Make shrinkable plastic book covers for your mini accordion book (see page 39).

☛ Create holiday ornaments with your own personal holiday greetings or memory on them along with photographs, drawings, etc.

☛ You can also make bookmarks, refrigerator magnets, zipper pulls, key chains, mobiles, and what-ever else your creative mind can come up with.

BINDING SOLUTIONS

Nothing makes a bunch of just-printed pages of a novel or story look better than a binding of some sort. Binding simply means attaching pages together to make a book. Here are four very simple ways to bind your novel, collection of stories, poems, or essays using unfolded pages. Perfect for computer-generated manuscripts.

WHAT YOU NEED

- Use of computer with printer or typewriter
- 8$\frac{1}{2}$ x 11-inch (21.6 x 27.9 cm) white printer paper (or paper of your choice)
- Your novel, short stories, or poems
- Paper clips
- Construction paper or poster board for front and back covers
- Scissors or craft knife
- Ruler and pencil
- Design materials to decorate the front cover
- Stapler with staples (for Staples and Tape Binding)
- Cloth-adhesive tape (for Staples and Tape Binding)
- Three-hole punch
- Looseleaf page (optional)
- Awl or nail (optional)
- 3 brass fasteners (for Brass Fastener Binding)
- 3 binder rings (for Binder Ring Binding)
- Yarn or long shoelace (for Simple Sewn Binding)

STAPLES AND TAPE BINDING

1. Before printing your writing, you may wish to place page numbers on each of the pages. Check your word-processing program to see how to do this, though in many programs, it's as easy as going to the main toolbar, clicking on "Insert," and then clicking on "Page Numbers."

2. After you've printed your piece, double-check the pages to make sure they printed correctly.

3. Gather all the pages together and line up their edges.

4. Hold the pages in place with paper clips.

5. Cut two pieces of construction paper $\frac{1}{4}$ inch (6 mm) larger than the pages on all four side.

6. Decorate your cover. Don't forget to include the title and your name.

7. Center the front cover on top of the pages. Center the bottom cover under the pages.

8. Staple down along the spine of the book about ½ inch (1.3 cm) from the edge.

9. Press a piece of cloth adhesive tape over the bound edge, covering the staples.

BRASS FASTENER BINDING

1. Follow steps 1 through 7 from the Staples and Tape Binding method on the previous page.

2. Use a three-hole punch to create the holes on the left-hand side of the manuscript. If you don't have a three-hole punch, mark the holes for the fasteners by placing a sheet of looseleaf paper on top of the front cover with the holes at the left side, leaving the ¼-inch (6 mm) border around the other three sides. Mark the hole positions with the pencil. Use an awl or nail to create the holes.

3. Decorate the cover. Push the fasteners through the holes from the front cover through the pages and the back cover. Then spread apart the fasteners' legs so they lie flat.

BINDER RINGS

Instead of brass fasteners, you can use individual binder rings. You can find them at craft and office supply stores.

SIMPLE SEWN BINDING

1. Follow steps 1 and 2 from the Brass Fastener Binding instructions on the previous page.

2. Pass the shoelace or yarn down through the center hole. Then pass it up through the top hole. Pass it down through the bottom hole. Then, up through the center hole. Pull the thread ends tight, then tie the ends together over the long top thread. Tie a knot or bow.

MAKING COPIES

You can make more than one copy of your bound book, of course, with the intention of either giving it to friends and family, or selling it. All you need to do is figure out how much it will cost to go to a copy center and make the copies, the supplies needed for the binding, and how many copies you want.

Where do you keep your writing ideas?

I keep a notebook that I use to write in, and my ideas usually end up in there.
—Caitlen Wood, age 13

Since I mostly find my ideas just before I fall asleep, I always have a sheet of paper on my desk so I can jot down ideas when I think of them. Sometimes, if worse comes to worse, I write them on my hand!
—Claire Moloney, age 12

In my head.
—Dana Tarr, age 11

In my writer's notebook.
—Devon Dickerson, age 9

If I am not in any place that I can write the story right there and then, I either make a mental note, or I try to find a piece of paper and I write it down.
—Emily Moloney, age 11

In my many notebooks.
—Hannah Currie, age 12

I keep my writing ideas in my top dresser draw, so that I have easy access to them.
—Jenny Spiegel, age 13

THE AWESOME ADVENTURES OF GNATBOY

by: K. Lee Evans

ALTERED BOOK

If you're not up for binding your own book, simply take an old novel, dictionary, or textbook and transform it into your own novel, story, or book of poems by gluing your words over the words already there. Then, decorate to your heart's content.

WHAT YOU NEED

- Old book (hardcover or paperback)
- Your writing
- Computer with printer
- White paint (optional)
- Scissors
- Decorative paper
- Glue stick and craft glue
- Markers
- Charms
- Rubber stamps and inks (optional)

WHAT YOU DO

1. There is no right or wrong way to create an altered book. They're never the same, so these instructions are just a starting point. The whole idea is to make the book unique and special, and it's okay to use any technique you can dream up.

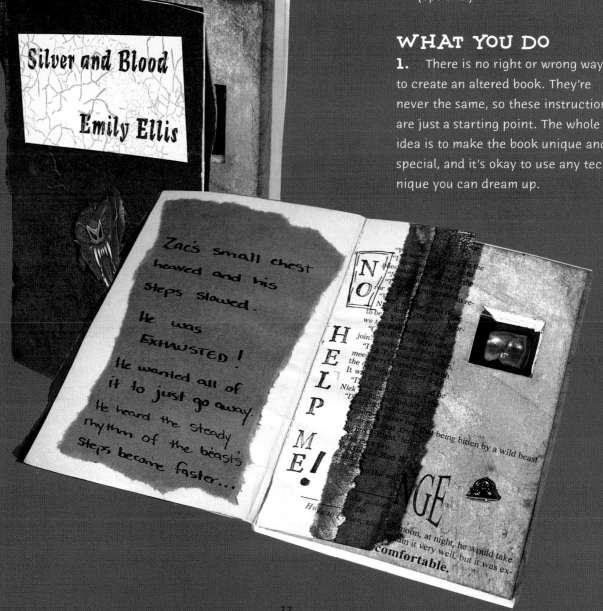

2. Design your cover. You can keep the cover as it is and only add your own name and title over the existing one, or cover the book cover with a piece of thick paper. Cut windows out of the paper if you want to show some of the old cover. Use stamps and card stock to create your title and name, or type them on the computer and choose a fun, readable font. The new title for this book was typed on a piece of card stock and glued to the new cover.

3. Type your story on the computer, and fix the margins so that the story will fit inside the book. Print test pages until you have the correct margins.

4. Cut the story out, and plan where you'd like to place it within the book.

5. Before gluing the story to the book, check out some of these techniques you can do to make the book look even cooler:

✎ Add or remove pages, cut out words, or paste in new ones.

✎ Paint out the words with white paint, and write in your story.

✎ Paste different paper over whole or partial pages, and write and draw on the pasted-on paper.

✎ If the original book has some words that work with your story, try covering a page with a piece of paper, then cutting away little rectangles that "reveal" the original words underneath.

✎ Tear pages in interesting ways, then write over them.

✎ Draw a picture that goes with the story over an existing page in the book.

✎ Glue in envelopes, then add little messages or "clues."

6. To create a shadow-box effect (see illustration below), glue together an entire section of pages, then cut out a window. Glue a charm, shell, found object, or other meaningful item to the next page in the book or to a separate piece of paper, then glue that paper to the window. You will think of many more ways to alter your book to suit the story you're creating.

Anything goes!

Silver and Blood

Emily Ellis

Silver and Blood

(excerpt)

Emily Ellis

"No...help me...!" Zac lurched forward as his toe caught the root of a tree. He skidded painfully on the uneven forest floor, fear clutching his stomach, making him sick. He had to get up quickly if there was any chance of survival. He scrambled awkwardly to his knees, tried to run, and lost his balance, crashing to the ground for the second time. Even a young boy like Zac knew he didn't have time to make a run for it. So he covered his head and curled into a ball on the hard ground. He barely had time to sob in his terror before the beast was on him. In a flash of teeth and blood, Zac lay in a crumpled heap, crying and bleeding, as the beast retreated into the depths of the night forest.

Even 30 years later, the incident was still fresh in Zac's mind.

Cover Blurbs

One way to get more people to read and/or buy your writing is to collect quotes from your admirers and show them off on the cover of your book. Give copies of your book to friends, family members, and teachers, and ask for their honest review of the work, in writing. Then, carefully read through the reviews and pick out the most memorable quotations, and copy them onto the front and back covers of your book. These quotations are called "blurbs," and a good blurb from someone respectable can really help potential readers decide to pick up your book. How important are blurbs? Book publishers jump for joy when someone like Stephen King or J.K. Rowling gives one of their books a great blurb. If you're really serious about publishing your book, consider sending it to a favorite writer. In most cases, you'll at least get a kind letter in reply. If you're really lucky, and your book blew your favorite writer away, he or she might give you a blurb.

Praise for:
SILVER AND BLOOD

"I was on the edge of my seat!"
    Amy, 3rd grade

"Too scary for words!"
    Jason, age 12

"Wow!"
    Mrs. Davis, 4th grade teacher

BRAINSTORMING

Give Little Red Riding Hood or some other classic children's picture book a complete makeover by simply adding your own words to go with the pictures. Paste over the old words with your new ones. You could also add details to the pictures. Change an ending you always hated. Let the bad guys win for once. Give the Seven Dwarfs some rollerblades. Whatever.

CALENDAR OF WORDS

Walk into any bookstore around the end of the year, and you'll find calendars commemorating everything from dogs, cars, and even chickens. So why not put all of your talents on display with a calendar of your own. Write seasonal poetry, celebrate birthdays for each month, or write poems for the holidays.

WHAT YOU NEED
- ✐ 24 pieces printer paper
- ✐ Computer
- ✐ Current calendar with next year's months in the back
- ✐ Ruler and pencil

- ✐ Markers, gel pens, or colored pencils
- ✐ 12 poems, stories, or a serial story (see page 38)
- ✐ Double-stick tape
- ✐ Hole punch (optional)

True Hero
By Paul Callahan

I have a dream, he said,
With thoughts of the later world in his head,
That one day this nation will rise up.
He wanted this world to be a peaceful place.

His birthday just passed, and we have to remember him.
He wanted things to be different from the way they had been.
He hoped that from now and forever after,
His children would be judged by their character.

Looking down on the world today,
What would Martin Luther King, Jr. say?
In these 30-plus years, through sorrow and tears,
We have faced and overcome our fears.

February

SUNDAY	MONDAY	TUESDAY	WEDNESDAY	THURSDAY	FRIDAY	SATURDAY
						1
2	3	4	5	6	7	8
9	10	11	12	13	14	15
16	17	18	19	20	21	22
23	24	25	26	27	28	

WHAT YOU DO

1. This project used 8½ x 11-inch (21.6 x 27.9 cm) paper, though you can create different sizes if you wish.

2. Create your months first. Many computers have programs for creating months. Try going to your "File Toolbar." Click "New" and look under "Other Documents." There might be a calendar program there. If so, simply follow the directions to create your months. If you don't have such a program, you can place the month of a current calendar under one of the pieces of paper, and with a pencil and ruler, trace the boxes. Then figure out the dates, days of the week, etc. for the month and year you're working on. Use markers, gel pens, or colored pencils to trace over the pencil marks for a cool look.

3. Once your months are done, it's time to create the designs for each month. Once you've matched your words for each month, you have many options for each month's design. You can work completely on the computer. Type your poem or story section, and import graphics as needed. Or, you can do it all by hand. You can create a collage with your words and images. The cloud image used in the background of the calendar page on the previous page is a digital image that was altered on a computer program. The calendar design on the right was also generated on a computer, but the moon was simply cut out and glued onto the page.

4. Once all the months are completed, create a cover for the calendar. Then, use the double-stick tape to adhere the cover page to January's image page. Make sure that the top of the cover page is attached to the bottom of January's page. Then glue January's calendar to February's image page, and so on, until it's all taped together.

5. Take your calendar to an office supply store or copy center to have it spiral bound. If you don't want to do that, you can hole punch the pages at the top and add ring binders. If you want, use the hole punch to create a hole through the calendar so it's easy to hang up.

Night
by Hannah Currie

Moonlight gently pushes itself, yet again, in to my life.
It creeps into my imagination
and stirs the soup of life.
As I glare at Moonlight,
I transform into a beast of the night.
Once the slender beams of Moonlight caress my heart,
I quietly become this creature
that grasps the moon like a jewel
and holds it tightly until the break of Dawn.

October

SUNDAY	MONDAY	TUESDAY	WEDNESDAY	THURSDAY	FRIDAY	SATURDAY
		1	2	3	4	5
6	7	8	9	10	11	12
13	14	15	16	17	18	19
20	21	22	23	24	25	26
27	28	29	30	31 HALLOWEEN		

Cliffhanger!

Tune in Next Time for the Exciting Conclusion!!!!!!

If you're looking to create a fun story for your calendar, consider writing a serial story. A serial is when you publish your story in installments and end each one with a cliffhanger. That's like when your hero is hanging from a cliff with hungry alligators below and a stagecoach full of bandits is barreling down the road toward him, and his arms are getting tired and his grip is starting to slip and...tune in next time—the chapter ends. Your readers are dying to know what happens next. How's he going to get out of this one? And, if you wrote a good enough cliffhanger, readers won't be able to think about anything else for the next two weeks (or however long it takes you to write the next installment). It's a good way to make sure they keep reading. Create a serial novella for your calendar, and leave each month's entry as a cliffhanger. Sure folks can read ahead, but tell them that's cheating.

ACCORDION BOOK

It's not quite a scroll; nor is it really a traditional book. What is it? An accordion fold book. You can turn the pages and read it, or stand it up and display it on a table. Pretty cool, eh!?

WHAT YOU NEED

- 8½ x 11-inch (21.6 x 27.9 cm) colored printer paper*
- Markers or colored pencils
- Pencil
- Scissors
- Card stock or poster board
- Glue
- Your poem or story

WHAT YOU DO

1. Decide what shape you want your book to be. It could be an animal, a geometric shape, or even a plain old rectangle. Whatever you want.

2. Fold a piece of 8½ x 11-inch (21.6 x 27.9 cm) scrap paper lengthwise. Draw the design on the folded paper, with the fold on the left-hand side. This will determine the size and shape of the whole book. Make sure you leave at least 4 inches (10.2 cm) of the fold uncut. Two inches (5.1 cm) on the other side needs to be straight to connect the folds later on (figure 1). Once you're happy with the design, cut it out. Notice you have two pages. Use this folded page as your template to create the book.

3. Decide how many pages you'll need to complete the book. If you think you need 20 pages, then fold 10

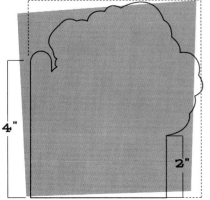

Figure 1

pieces of the colored paper in half the same way you folded the scrap paper. Place your template over the first page with the folds matched up, and draw the outline of the template lightly with the pencil. Cut out the outline—you now have one spread. Repeat with the rest of the pages until you have the number of spreads you want.

4. Trace the template's outline onto the two pieces of thin cardboard. Cut them out. These will be your front and back covers.

5. Stack your pages inside the covers to make sure it looks good.

6. Glue one spread to the front cover.

7. Cut a piece of the colored paper into several $\frac{1}{2}$ x 2-inch (1.3 x 5.1 cm) tabs. These will be glued to the spreads to create the accordion fold.

8. Connect the first spread you attached to the front cover to another spread by gluing one tab where the two spreads connect (figure 2). Repeat this until your book is done.

9. Design your covers, and write your words in the book in pencil. Check for errors, and then go over the words with a marker. Add spreads if you need to. (That's why you haven't attached the back cover yet.)

10. Once you've finished with the words, glue the last spread to the back cover.

Songbird
Jenny Spiegel

A songbird sitting way up in a tree,
Why, oh why, why couldn't that be me?
Up so high, not a care in the world.
I might be blue or pretty as a pearl.
Singing sweet songs all through the day,
Listen closer and you might hear me say:

A little girl way down on the ground,
There is no way I can live there, I've found.
For I must stay here, up in the trees,
And she may roam wherever she'd please.
I wish I could live in a grand house like that.
Then I would never be chased by the cat.

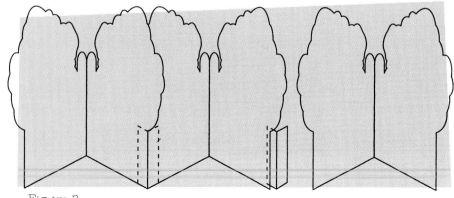

Figure 2

40

LITERARY LUMINARY

During the day, it's a mild-mannered piece of paper painted and folded into a box. But at night, light the candle, turn off the lights, and let your words glow.

WHAT YOU NEED

- ✎ Mulberry paper, rice paper, or any other paper that is appropriate for watercolor paints and allows light to shine through
- ✎ Scissors
- ✎ Ruler and pencil
- ✎ Watercolor paints
- ✎ Paintbrush
- ✎ Carbon paper
- ✎ Tissue paper
- ✎ Ballpoint pen
- ✎ Glue
- ✎ Candle
- ✎ Votive holder

WHAT YOU DO

1. Cut a piece of paper at least 22 inches (55.9 cm) long and 10 inches (25.4 cm) wide.

2. Fold this paper in half lengthwise.

3. Fold both ends of the paper in approximately ¹/₂ inch (1.3 cm) to create two lips where you'll eventually glue the paper together (see figure 1 on page 42).

4. Fold the entire piece of paper in half again lengthwise. When you unfold the paper, this will give you

41

the four sections of your luminary (figure 1).

5. Spread the paper on a flat surface and create your design lightly with the pencil. Before using the watercolors, practice on some scrap paper first. Colors will spread on the paper depending on how much water you add to the paint.

6. As you're laying out and painting your design, remember to consider how it will look when folded and standing up. Pay attention to the creases that you created when you folded the paper, and consider using lighter colors where you want the words to shine through. You can also glue shapes and stickers to the inside of the luminary, or poke small holes in the paper with a thumbtack to allow the light to shine out.

7. Once the paint has dried thoroughly, it's time to add words to your piece of art. Lay the luminary paper on the piece of carbon paper

so that the carbon paper is ink-side up and facing the side of the paper without the artwork on it (figure 2).

8. Place the piece of tissue paper on top of the luminary paper where you want the words to appear.

9. Place a copy of your words over the tissue paper, and, pressing down as hard as you can, trace your words. As you write, the carbon paper will transfer the words to the underside of the luminary (see

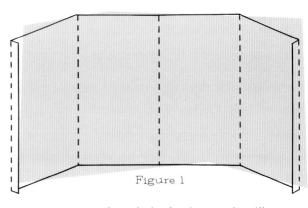

Figure 1

photo below). The words will appear backwards, but will look right from the outside when the candle shines from within.

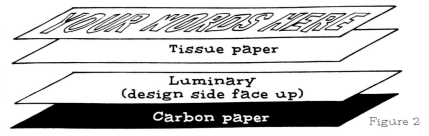

Figure 2

10. With your creases as a guide, refold the paper and glue the two inside lips to create the box.

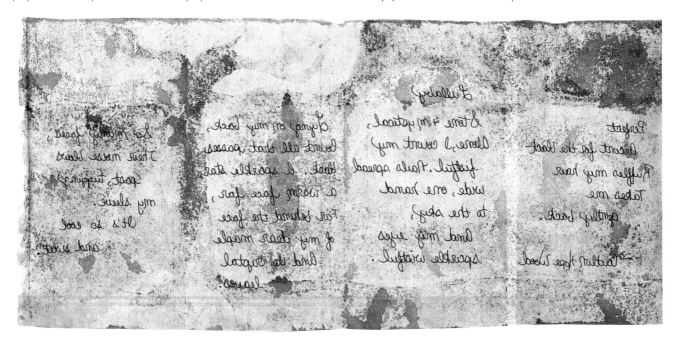

11. Place the luminary over the votive candle. Make sure the luminary is centered around the votive and not too close to the paper. Don't leave the candle lit if you leave the room, and don't make your luminary any smaller than the dimensions noted in step 1.

Lullaby
Caitlin Hope Wood

Stone and mystical,
Alone I count my fistful.
Nails spread wide, one hand
  to the sky,
And my eyes sparkle wistful.
Lying on my back,
Count all that passes black.
A sparkle star, a warm face
  far,
Far behind the face of my
  dear maple
And its crystal leaves.
So many faces,
Their noise blows past,
  tugging my sleeve.
It's so cool and sweet.
Perfect
Accent for the black—
Ruffles my hair,
Takes me gently back.

Where's your favorite place to write?

I like to write in the kitchen because it's usually warm, and it's comforting. Noise doesn't bother me that much, but if it does, or my family is interrupting me, I go to my room instead.
—Alex Cole-Weiss, age 13

My favorite place to write would have to be in my room. I really like the feeling of being in bed and writing. It's just so comfortable.
—Anna Godden, age 12

My favorite place to write is either in my room or upstairs in front of the sliding glass doors looking out onto the ocean. I feel it is easier to write anything when all you hear is your breathing and the sound of ink being placed on paper with your own words. The ocean inspires me to write something truly special.
—Emily Moloney, age 11

I like to go outside, preferably under a tree or at the beach. Outside everything is so peaceful and connected that you can't help getting inspired by its glory.
—Chelsea Smith, age 13

How do you get over "writer's block?"

I write something really strange and it sometimes turns out pretty good.
—Adam Rush, age 12

I leave the subject alone for awhile and think about something else.
—Alex Cole-Weiss, age 13

If I can't think of what to write, or my story is going nowhere, I just stop and take a break—anywhere from five minutes to a week. However, if a story is due for school, I try to either come up with a new idea that would be easier, or I try to sit and let my mind relax, so I am not so tense.
—Claire Moloney, age 12

BOOK ON TAPE

Are you finding that family members are too busy to read your newest novel? Do you have a relative or neighbor who has trouble seeing type on a page? Bone up on your storytelling skills, and record your novel, poems, or stories on audio tape.

WHAT YOU NEED

- ✎ Audio tape with tape box
- ✎ Tape recorder
- ✎ Your writing
- ✎ Sound effects
- ✎ Construction paper
- ✎ Scissors
- ✎ Design materials

WHAT YOU DO

1. Find a quiet and comfortable place to work. Record yourself reading one page of your story. Play it back. Are you reading too quickly? Too slowly? Keep practicing until you feel you've got it right. If you want, go to the library and check out an audio book to get the feel of how to read your story.

Basically, you should read with feeling. Get into the story and practice using different voices when reading dialog. You don't have to mimic the voices exactly, just practice making sure they sound a little bit different.

2. Though totally optional, you may wish to add simple sound effects. This could be a challenge to coordinate, and you may need an assistant. (A friend or younger sibling would work just fine). Sound effects usually sound sort of funny on tape, so you may not want to include them in a

very serious piece (see below for some pointers).

3. Once you're satisfied you've got the right tempo, voice, sound effects, and assistants, begin recording. First state the name of the story and its author (you). You could also add a dedication (whom the book is dedicated to) and a brief description of the book. Pause recording. Turn to your first chapter, clear your throat, and record. Press pause at the end of paragraphs when you need a break, and if you mess up, rewind to a point where there's a natural break, and start re-reading from there.

4. Once you're done recording for the day, turn off the tape recorder, and mark exactly where you stopped reading.

5. Read ahead for the next session. What simple sound effects (if any) could you include for your next recording session?

6. Once you're done recording, mark the title and author of the story on the label on the tape, and decorate and cut out a tape cover. Use a tape-to-tape recorder to make copies.

COOL, EASY SOUND EFFECTS

☛ Scrape the teeth of a comb with a fingernail for a cricket sound.

☛ Sprinkle salt on aluminum foil for light rainfall.

☛ Clop two coconut halves on a wooden board for the sound of horses galloping.

☛ Twist cellophane for a crackling fire.

☛ Blow through a straw into water for the sound of boiling water.

☛ Scratch paper with an unbent paper clip for the sound of writing.

☛ Shake a piece of sheet metal for thunder.

☛ Sprinkle some cornstarch on the floor, then walk across it, for the sound of someone walking on snow.

☛ Electronic keyboards usually have cool buttons with fun sounds on them.

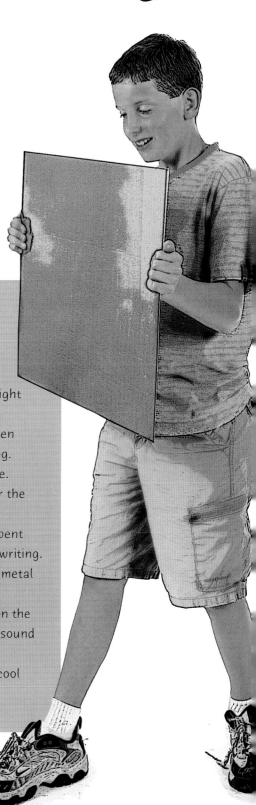

MAGNETIC WORDS

Print a familiar nursery rhyme or saying on magnetic paper, stick the words to a tin, and rearrange them to make new poems anytime, anywhere. Once you've got a poem you love, place the words somewhere metallic where people can read them: your bike, the refrigerator, a metal picture frame, etc.

WHAT YOU NEED
- Computer and printer
- Printer compatible magnetic paper*
- Scissors
- Old tin
- Dust mask
- Gloves
- Sandpaper, 120 grit
- Damp rag

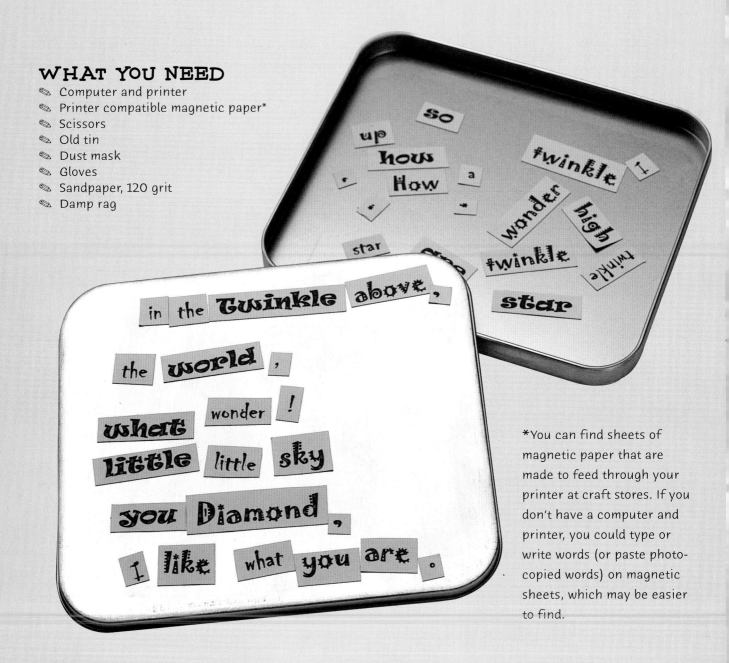

*You can find sheets of magnetic paper that are made to feed through your printer at craft stores. If you don't have a computer and printer, you could type or write words (or paste photocopied words) on magnetic sheets, which may be easier to find.

WHAT YOU DO

1. Look for poems, nursery rhymes, even advertising copy that has inspiring words you'd like to rearrange to form new poems and sayings. For this project, the words from that old nursery rhyme "Twinkle, Twinkle Little Star" were used.

2. Type the words you've chosen in a fun font. Insert two spaces between each word you type and leave one and a half spaces between lines so it'll be easier to cut the words from the magnetic paper later on. Also type a bunch of punctuation marks. Adjust the document margins so that they measure 1/2 inch (1.3 cm) on all sides of the page, so you can make the most of each page of magnetic paper.

3. Print the page of words and punctuation marks onto a plain piece of printer paper and check for spaces, cut-off words, and any other problems you should fix before you print on the magnetic paper.

4. Set a sheet of magnetic paper in the tray, positioned so the white side of the paper will be printed on. If you're not sure if the white side should face up or down in the tray, do a test run with a piece of scrap paper. Make an X on the paper, put the paper in the tray so the X is facing up, and print the page of words to see which side comes out blank and which gets printed on.

5. Use scissors to cut the words from the magnetic paper. Save leftover scraps of the magnetic paper for other projects.

6. Wear a dust mask and gloves while you sand the surface of the tin to remove old paint and dirt. When you're happy with the way the tin looks, wipe it clean with the damp rag.

7. Fill the tin with the magnetic words. Stick words to the cover of the tin and rearrange them to make new poems. Add new words to the tin from time to time for fresh vocabulary.

BRAINSTORMING

Create your own bumper stickers for the family car. Use magnetic sheets and glue your bumper sticker words to them. Make sure they're big enough for everyone to read. Spray the words with clear acrylic sealer so they'll hold up better when it rains.

MOOD MOBILE

Not sure how you're feeling today? Create this mobile to express your ever-changing moods. Not only can you write on both sides of the mobile pieces, but you can also erase your writing and start over.

WHAT YOU NEED

- White construction paper
- Tissue paper, assorted colors
- Scissors
- Lamination paper* or clear self-adhesive shelf paper
- Waxed dental floss
- Needle
- Beads
- 3 to 5 wooden dowels, ¼ inch diameter (6 mm), 12 inches (30.5 cm) long
- Acrylic paint
- Paintbrush
- String
- White glue and water
- Small paintbrush
- Your words
- Dry-erase marker
- Eraser or damp cloth
  *Available at craft stores. Lamination paper comes in rolls, and you simply cut out what you need.

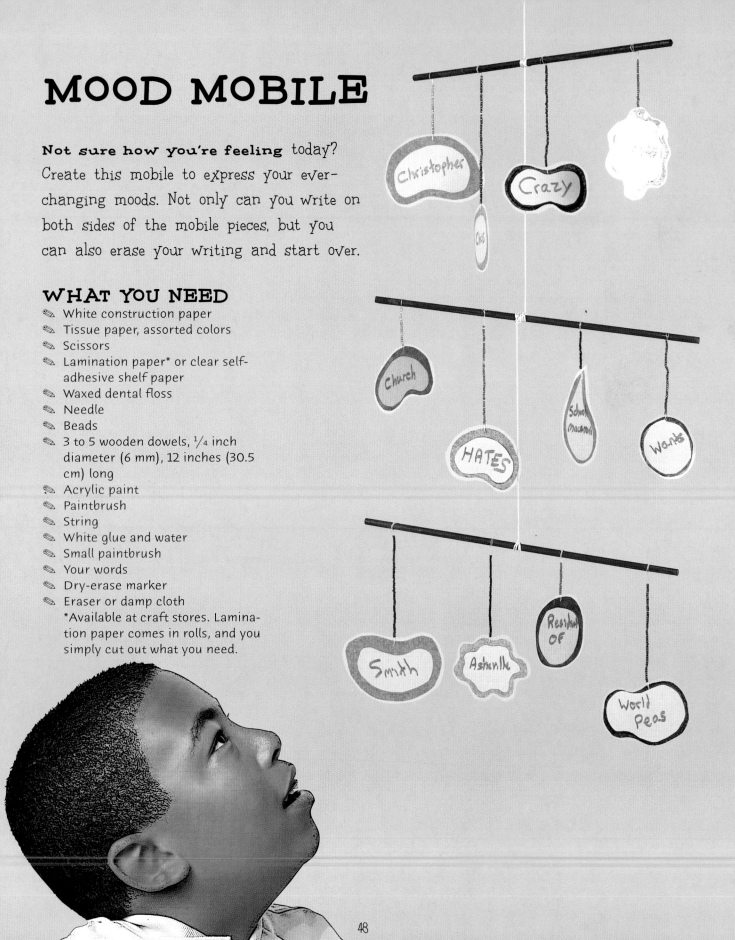

WHAT YOU DO

1. Cut out squares of construction paper and tissue paper.

2. Make a tissue paper sandwich by putting a piece of tissue paper between two pieces of construction paper. Cut the sandwich into the desired shape and size.

3. Remove the tissue paper, and set it aside. Trim the pieces of construction paper so that there will be a tissue paper "frame" around the construction paper on each side (see photo detail below).

4. Peel away the backing of the laminate, and press one construction paper cutout on the sticky side of the laminate. Place the tissue paper on top of the construction paper and your second piece of paper on top of the tissue paper. Peel the backing from a second piece of laminate, and press it on top of your construction and tissue paper. Trim around your piece, leaving a border of laminate around the edges of the frame. Repeat for the number of pieces you want for your mobile.

5. Cut off a length of waxed dental

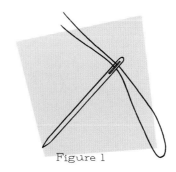

Figure 1

floss. The floss will be used to attach the pieces to the mobile, so determine how long you want the floss to be. Vary the lengths if you want.

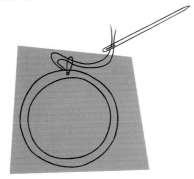

Figure 2

6. Thread both ends of the floss through the needle (figure 1). Pass the needle through the top edge of one of your laminated pieces. Create a loop with the floss, and pass the needle through the looped end (figure 2).

Figure 3

7. Thread beads onto the dental floss through the needle. Make sure you leave enough floss at the end to tie it to the dowel later (figure 3).

8. Place the mobile piece aside carefully, and repeat steps 5 through 7 for each piece.

9. To create the mobile, first paint the dowels. After they've dried, attach the dowels with string. Make sure to leave enough string above the top dowel so you can hang the mobile when you're done.

10. Carefully tie each mobile piece to the dowels by tying the two ends of the beaded dental floss into a knot.

11. Hang the mobile and move things around until it's balanced. Cut any loose ends of string on the mobile. Dilute some glue with water, and brush the loose ends of string with glue to make them lie flat on the surface of the dowel. This also keeps the pieces of the mobile from sliding all over the dowels.

12. Write your words with a dry-erase marker so you can erase them with a damp paper towel later on.

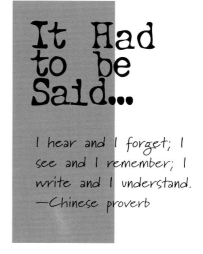

It Had to be Said...

I hear and I forget; I see and I remember; I write and I understand.
—Chinese proverb

"EAT YOUR WORDS"

Well, no, you won't actually be eating your words, but you'll be eating ON your words with these easy and fun projects. Create several place mats and dinnerware with different poems or sections of a story, and use them at home, sell them at a craft fair, or give them as gifts.

I am a Horse

Emily Ellis

I am a horse with grace and a sweet face,
With power that works every day, every hour
With heart that never dies, with a spirit that always flies,
With deep brown eyes,
With beauty that strikes man like lightening,
With powerful hooves that seem quite frightening.
I am a horse that has helped man for ages.
I'll even help him in mad rages.

FOR THE PLACE MATS

What You Need

- Scrap paper and pencil
- Poster board (optional)
- Decorative paper
- Collage items related to writing
- Scissors
- Glue
- Your writing
- Gel pen or marker
- Lamination paper or clear self-adhesive shelf paper (optional)

What You Do

1. Design your place mats on scrap paper first. Play with different techniques. The photographed place mat uses four different pieces of decorative paper to give the illusion of sky, mountains, and clouds, along with an image that relates to the poem.

2. Cut a piece of poster board or paper to the size of your place mat.

3. Arrange the other elements of your design, and glue them to the poster board or paper. In the place mat shown here, the different papers were simply layered on top of each other.

4. Carefully copy your writing onto the place mat with the pencil first. Then, copy over the words with the gel pen or marker.

5. Once your place mat design is done, create more if you want. Then, either bring the placemats to an office-supply store to have them laminated, or laminate yourself with the shelf paper.

6. To laminate the placemats yourself, cut a piece of the lamina-tion or shelf paper slightly larger than the place mats. Peel off the backing and place it sticky side up onto your work surface.

7. Carefully lay the place mat on the paper and smooth it down.

8. Cut a second piece and place it on top of the place mat.

9. Cut around the edges of the place mat until the lamination or shelf paper is the same length around the mat.

FOR THE DINNERWARE

What You Need

- Pencil
- Paper
- Your writing

What You Do

1. You don't have to set up your own ceramics studio to do this project. Simply check around town for the nearest ceramics studio. They'll have everything you'll need. Look in the phone directory under such headings as arts and crafts, art instruction, ceramics, clay, crafts, glazes, kiln, pottery, and studios. Call your local Chamber of Commerce if you don't have any luck with a listing—most likely, you'll find a studio within driving distance.

2. When contacting these studios, ask them what kind of pottery

pieces they have available, how much they charge, how long it takes to get your piece back after it has been fired in the kiln, and whether or not it's okay to bring your own stamps, brushes, and stencils.

3. Plan out your design as much as possible before going to the studio. Once at the studio, choose the pieces you want to work with.

marks will disappear in the kiln and leave no trace. So, don't worry about making mistakes, you don't even have to erase them.

5. Once you have your design penciled in, use the paints the studio has to offer. Afterwards, the pieces will be placed in a liquid glaze and baked in a kiln that melts and fuses the glaze onto the pieces. All that's left to do is pick up your pieces when they're ready.

paints, you can wash them off and start over.

☛ Develop a theme for a set of dinnerware pieces, such as the stars and wavy lines in the projects shown here.

☛ Don't forget to sign your name under the pieces. You can also write special messages if the dinnerware is meant as a gift.

with excitement and fear. Could it fly?

...ld fly, all right ! ...ghtest little tug and ...up 50 feet at 30 mph.

I got down as quickly as I could without freaking.

4. Write your words and draw your designs directly on the pieces with the pencil before painting. Pencil

TIPS:

☛ Select a small paintbrush for the letters.

☛ Lighter colors, such as yellow, will blend into the white background, so consider adding a second coat after the first one dries.

☛ If you make a mistake with the

Riley's Magic Carpet Ride
Riley Hurst

I was camping with Calum and Paul, and I sat down and felt something soft. It was a magic flying carpet. We decided to test it right then.

The next minute I was trembling with excitement and fear. Could it fly? It could fly, all right! The slightest little tug and it shot up 50 feet at 30 mph. I got down as quickly as I could without freaking.

Then, we were off again. Our destination: home. On the way, we flew over vast forests. We decided we would keep the carpet at my house and promised not tell anyone.

WHAT WRITERS WRITE

Writing isn't just for books. Writers work for magazines, television, radio, movies, websites, stage...you name it. Here's a list of just some of the things writers such as yourself can write:

autobiography
advertisement
advice
  column
biography
book
  review
brochure
cartoon
CD review
    comic strip
    cookbook
      dialogue play
      diary
        editorial
        essay
          fairy tale
          fantasy
          feature
    article
greeting card
history
instructions
interview
kid's book
letter to
  the editor
letter
memoir
myth
magazine
  article

movie review
mystery
myth
newspaper
  column
novel
novella
opinion
oral history
parody
play
play review
poetry
profile
puppet show
radio play
report on current
  events
researched report
romance
science fiction
screenplay
script
short story
skit
speech
textbook: how to
tribute
tv review
tv script
web page

MINI-BOOK NECKLACE

With this project, your words will not only affect people and perhaps help change the world, but they'll also become an awesome fashion statement.

WHAT YOU NEED

- 8½ x 11-inch (21.6 x 27.9 cm) piece of paper
- Ruler and pencil
- Scissors
- Manila file folder
- Colored pencils, crayons, or markers
- Stapler
- Your poem
- Glue stick
- Awl or thin nail
- Ribbon
- Silver paper (optional)
- Star-shaped paper punch (optional)

WHAT YOU DO

1. Measure and cut a 2¼ x 10½-inch (5.7 x 26.7 cm) strip from the piece of paper.

2. Measure in 1½ inches (3.8 cm) from one end of the long paper strip. Fold the strip at this point. Continue accordion folding the strip, making each panel the same size. Fold neatly, and crease each fold well. Set this aside for now.

3. Measure and cut a rectangle measuring 2- x 4½ inches (6 x 11.4 cm) from the manila file folder.

4. Decorate one side of the rectangle. This will be the outside or cover of the booklet. This project was decorated with metallic colored pencils.

5. Using figure 1 as a guide, mark and fold the rectangle at the lines indicated (with the decorated side out). Cut the corners as seen in figure 1.

6. Staple once just above the short fold line (figure 2).

7. Write your poem or story on the accordion folded paper, or use the computer to print it out, then glue small sections to each page of the booklet.

8. Glue the accordion-folded booklet inside the folded cover. The longer front flap will tuck into the shorter one when the book is closed (like a matchbook).

9. With the awl or nail, punch a hole in the center of the narrow spine at the top of the book (the space between the back cover and front flap) (see figure 2).

10. Cut a length of ribbon long enough to fit over your head. Tie the ends together.

11. Thread the ribbon through the hole from the inside out. The knot will catch on the inside of the book. You can also punch stars from silver paper, and glue them onto the cover of the book.

Reddy the Fox's Favorite Star

Dana Tarr

Reddy the Fox had a very favorite star.
He would wish on that star.
Sometimes he would write a story
of the adventures they would have
  someday.
It made him happy;
it made him sad to think about his
  friend.
He wished he could reach up and
grab his friend right out of the sky
and take him away forever.

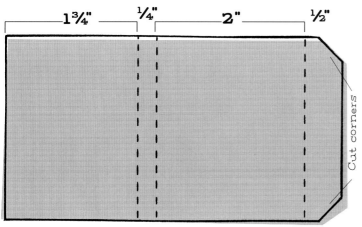

Figure 1

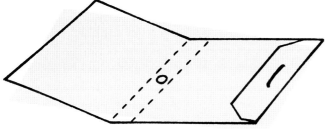

Figure 2

BRAINSTORMING

Did you know that **Green Eggs and Ham** would have never been written if it weren't for a bet? A friend bet Dr. Seuss that he couldn't write a book with only 50 different words in it. Dr. Seuss won the bet with **Green Eggs and Ham**. According to rumor, he never got his money.

The next time you're stumped, create some writing challenges for yourself. Can you create a short story that fits in the Mini-Book Necklace? Can you write a poem in which you don't repeat any words? How about a book with only 83 words?

ROCK & WIRE POETRY HOLDERS

These simple holders look great on a shelf, mantel, or anywhere somebody would see them. Display your poems, photos, postcards, and even your writing to-do list. And instead of rocks, you can use driftwood or other weighty treasures.

Loved by a River

As I knelt by the river
I looked deep within—
Down to the depths
and the shallows,
I saw love—
Love in the purest form:
Ungiven, untouched,
untaken, underestimated
by far.
For there is no love
like the river's.

A river can remember
the color of your eyes
When the world has forgotten
your name.
A river will cherish your face
for a thousand years or more.
I am loved by a river

Poem Ideas!
- Tree that Grandma planted
- Smelly gym clothes
- Hike on Rattlesnake Ridge

WHAT YOU NEED

- Needle-nose wire cutters
- 16-gauge wire
- Favorite rocks
- Your writing, neatly written or typed on small sturdy pieces of paper or card stock

WHAT YOU DO

1. Cut a length of wire about 18 to 24 inches (45.7 x 61 cm) depending on the size of your rock.

2. Using the pliers and your fingers, create a card "holder" by coiling or bending one end of the wire into a shape that will hold paper. Keep a paper clip nearby to refer to.

3. Decide which side of the rock will be the bottom of the holder.

Wrap and twist the wire tightly around the rock. Adjust and check the wire placement by setting the rock on a level surface to make sure the rock doesn't wobble. You'll probably have to have two wraps under the rock so it sits level. After the rock is wrapped in the wire, bend the end of the wire around the holder end of the wire.

4. Make minor adjustments to your wire shape, and tighten it all up with the pliers. Insert your poetry.

SCROLL IT

Around 5,000 years ago, the Egyptians discovered that they could use papyrus to write on. However, there was one slight problem. You can't fold papyrus. Being the resourceful people that they were, the Egyptians created scroll books. If you think your story is too long to scroll, just know that some ancient scrolls are over 150 feet (45 m) long.

WHAT YOU NEED

- Your story, essay, or long poem
- Computer and printer
- Colored printer paper
- Scissors
- Ruler
- Glue
- Two tiny decorative pencils or other objects (optional)
- Round candy tin
- Construction paper

WHAT YOU DO

1. Type your story on the computer. Edit and proofread it, and then decide what font size and type you want to use. Choose a font size that's not too big for the tin. If you don't have a computer, either type or handwrite the story on colored paper.

2. Print the story onto the colored printer paper. Use different colored paper for each page if you want.

3. Cut the story into strips that are the same height. Use the ruler to check the height of each strip before cutting. Also make sure

the strips will fit in the tin with the lid closed.

4. Glue the strips together to form the scroll.

5. Glue small objects to the beginning and end of the scroll if you want.

6. Trace the outline of the lid onto a piece of construction paper. Draw your cover design in the circle you just drew. Cut the circle out, and glue it to the lid. Place the scroll in the tin.

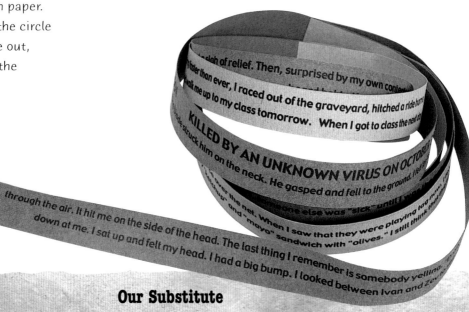

Our Substitute

Ty deVries

It was October 31, 2001, and our teacher, Mr. Justice, was away. We had a substitute that day. To describe him the best that I can will be difficult. He was just...different. We had a couple of weeks like no other. Here's how it went.

When I walked in the door at 8:50 I saw our substitute sitting rigid in my seat.

"Excuse me." I tapped him on the shoulder. "Will you please find another chair? My feet are killing me."

Then, I saw a switch right below one of the probes on the left side of his neck. It said, "Flip to activate."

Of course, out of my own curiosity, I flipped it. I wish I hadn't.

The result was flickers of electricity from the probes to his head. After several seconds of lightning flickering, a strong bolt—strong enough to knock someone out—shot out from the probes. Our substitute twitched violently. Slowly, he stood up and looked straight down at me. He was about 7' 6" tall.

"What's your name?" I asked.

He walked over to the dry-erase board and wrote in messy handwriting, "Frank N. Stein."

"So. What do you want us to call you?" I asked.

He took the eraser and erased "Frank N." and wrote "Mr."

"So, you want us to call you Mr. Stein?"

He grunted to show approval. Right then it turned 9:00. The students came piling in. They stopped dead in their tracks when they saw Mr. Stein. Some were sniggering. Others were whispering. By the time they stopped, Mr. Stein looked like he had just about had enough. When the class was seated, I noticed that Allijah was missing. Zack said that he was sick.

Once we were settled, Mr. Stein pointed toward the door. Zack and I exchanged puzzled looks, shrugged, and lined up. The rest of the class followed suit. When we got to the bottom of the stairs, Mr. Stein stopped abruptly. We all crashed into the person in front of us. He walked to the back of the line. I looked back at him. He gave me a look that clearly meant, "go." Without thinking, I raced through the front door, through the gate, and got to the tetherball first. The first person I challenged was Wilkin. He beat me during the 10-second countdown. He challenged everybody present in the class. He beat them all.

Having more confidence, he challenged Mr. Stein. Wilkin got the ball first. After the drop, he hit it hard. It went straight to Mr. Stein—hard. Mr. Stein hit it—hard. The ball went flying through the air. It hit me on the side of the head. The last thing I remember is somebody yelling, "Draw!"

I woke up to see five or six people looking down at me. I sat up and felt my head. I had a big bump. I looked between Ivan and Zev to see a five-foot wide "crater" in the server's spot on the volley-ball court. I guessed that Mr. Stein had slammed the ball full force over the net. When I saw that they were playing tag now, I felt like fainting again.

When we went in for lunch, I saw that Mr. Stein had a soggy "ketchup" and "mayo" sandwich with "olives." I still think that the sandwich was pus and blood and green eyeballs.

Mr. Stein substituted for the next 11 days. Each of those days, someone else was "sick" until I was the only one left. On that day, I started to go out for recess, but Mr. Stein grabbed my shoulder and stopped me right there. He walked me for two miles to a cemetery. He pointed to a rusty shovel lying on the ground. I picked it up and automatically started to sink my shovel into the dirt. He stopped me by loudly grunting. He pointed to the grave to the right of the one that I started on. I was beginning to start to dig but then I saw the name engraved on the headstone.

ALLIJAH MOTIKA
BORN 1991
DIED 2001
KILLED BY AN UNKNOWN VIRUS
ON OCTOBER 31st

Not knowing what to do, I swung the shovel at Mr. Stein. The blade struck him on the neck. He gasped and fell to the ground. I felt for his pulse in all the places I knew—nothing. I was certain that he was dead.

Heart beating faster than ever, I raced out of the graveyard, hitched a ride home, and ran inside to tell my mom what had happened. She said that she would walk me up to my class tomorrow.

When I got to class the next day, my heart felt like it did a som-ersault when I saw everyone there. I breathed out a sigh of relief. Then, surprised by my own con-tentedness, my stomach dropped when I saw Mr. Justice smiling maliciously with the word Tardy on the dry-erase board behind him.

WHY SO SHY?

Emily Dickinson wrote 1,775 poems. (If you wanted to write that many poems, you'd have to write one a day for nearly five years.) And though that's not a world record, there are two remarkable things to know about Emily and her poetry:

Fact #1: Most of Emily's poems were awesome.

Fact #2: Only a couple of Emily's poems were ever published while she was alive. In fact, she hated the thought of seeing her words in print. The few that were published were done anonymously and against her will. (Emily was, however, supposedly fond of sending a poem to neighbors along with a homemade cake.)

Luckily for us, after Emily died, her sister found an old box full of her poetry. She had none of Emily's reservations about seeing them in print, and decided to publish every single one of them.

Top 10 Poetry Whoppers Exposed!

Your teacher walks into the classroom, brimming with excitement, and exclaims, "Today we start our unit on writing and reading...poetry!" A collective sigh escapes from the classroom. Some students make a break for the door. One student screams, "No, anything but that! Please, I'm allergic."

Poetry! I'm outta here!

Why do kids (and many adults) fear poetry? One reason is that they think poetry ABSOLUTELY must be painful. It MUST be hard to understand, and even more difficult to write. Lies! Lies! All lies!

1. All poems are boring. (Only boring poems are boring.)

2. All poems are mushy stuff about Greek gods and flowers and birds and love. (Poems can be about anything: dump trucks, black socks, you name it.)

3. All poems must rhyme. (Just plain wrong. If this were true, you'd have to take away almost all of today's poets' licenses to write poetry—okay, so there's no such thing, but you get my point.)

4. All poems use difficult words. (That's a total prevarication.)

5. All poems are puzzles written in code in order to make you feel stupid. (No, though it pays to take your time when reading a poem since every word counts. And poems tend to relate to experiences you feel, taste, smell, etc.)

6. All poems are written by old men in tweed jackets and can't be written by people such as yourself. (Tweed jackets are uncomfortable, and one of North America's bestselling poets in recent memory was an 11-year-old boy.)

7. Poems are very serious business. (Read Shel Silverstein and Jack Prelutsky.)

8. You need to be specially trained to write poetry. (You can start right now. No diploma necessary.)

9. Writing a poem is always a hard and painful experience. (Sure it can be hard getting the words just right, but that goes for ANY kind of writing.)

10. All poems are in lines and metered. (Read e.e. cummings.)

ENOUGH SAID. GET OUT THERE AND GIVE POETRY A TRY.

READING IN THE RAIN

Make a splash with this umbrella that will show off your words and keep you dry at the same time.

WHAT YOU NEED

- Black umbrella
- Scrap paper and pencil
- Your words
- Thin paintbrush
- Letter stencils (optional)
- Newspaper
- Hardcover book
- Bought or homemade stamp
- Acrylic paints
- Plastic plate (to mix paints)
- Foam brush

WHAT YOU DO

1. Open up the umbrella. Create your design on scrap paper. Carefully consider where you're going to put the words and whether or not you have enough room for them. If not, either find a bigger umbrella, or edit.

2. Copy your words onto the umbrella with the acrylic paint. Let the words dry overnight. Use stencils if you want.

3. Tear a piece of newspaper large enough to cover the top of your book, and place the covered book inside the opened umbrella behind the area that you want to stamp.

4. If you're making your own stamp, see page 15. Squeeze out a small amount of paint onto the plastic plate, and use the foam brush to "ink" the stamp with the paint.

5. First stamp onto a piece of scrap paper. Adjust if the stamp is too dark or light. If it looks good, press the stamp evenly onto the umbrella's surface with good pressure. Make sure the book is under the stamp as you do this. Keep all of your stamping between the seam lines.

6. Add other painted decorations if you want. Allow the umbrella to dry for a day or two before using.

Hopscotch Puddle Jump

K. Lee Evans

Hopscotch puddle jump,
leap into the air.
Land upon a toadstool cloud.
Look, it's raining down there!

61

POETRY LIGHTBOX

Use a small cardboard mailing box or recycle a snack box to create a decorative frame that not only stands upright, but also sheds some light on your words.

A Pawn, I advance & don't draw back. I am forever ready to die. Banner raised high, I have no fear. Nobly ready to die. I stand straight in my saddle. MEN + horses fall. Don't give me a hassle. I am the Bishop greed + slave or free, better than ye. The one who has the power of white, I say or sin. Arrows shoot, the one who has the Pawn to the front, whose king running. I keep the King the Queen who can make any move who has the King to do my whining, I can adore the Rook, the castle. I am the King, bow down on his knee. I am keep the Knight. I go forward into battle. A Knight I am, higher than all Knight Moving, I king moving, of subjects to a fight.

WHAT YOU NEED

- Small, sturdy cardboard box
- Scissors or craft knife
- Wrapping paper
- Design materials
- White craft glue and water
- Foam brush
- Adhesive-backed hook-and-loop tape*
- Pocket flashlight
- Your writing
- White paper
- Tape

*Available at craft stores

WHAT YOU DO

1. When choosing a box to use, make sure the box can stand up on its own. A small flashlight will be attached to the inside back wall of this box, so keep that in mind when deciding.

2. Use the scissors or craft knife to cut the bottom off the box. Make sure the box stands up straight.

3. Decide what kind of window you want for the box. Use the scissors or craft knife to cut out the window. Make sure the window is big enough for your poem.

4. Decoupage the box with wrapping paper and magazine cut-outs (see page 16). You can also paint the box if you want; and after the box dries, attach buttons, small pieces of balsa wood cut into various shapes, rhinestones, beads, and anything else that strikes your fancy.

5. Cut a few strips of the hook-and-loop tape, and stick them to the inside center of the back of your box. Attach the other pieces to the back of a pocket flashlight. Try to find a flat flashlight that has a halogen lightbulb.

6. Print, handwrite, or stamp your writing on the white paper, and tape it to the inside of the window so the words are facing out. Turn on the flashlight, and stand the box up.

On Angel's Wings
Fly me to safety.
Fly me to care.
Fly me to love.
Fly me to trust.
Fly me to faith.
Fly me to joy, hope
and happiness
On Angel's wings fly...

Kingdom

Adam Rush

A Pawn, I advance and don't draw back.
I am forever ready to attack.
I go forward into battle.
A Knight I am, I sit straight in my saddle.
Banner raised high,
I have no fear—nobly ready to die!
Standing high and tall, I am higher than all.
Arrows shoot; men and horses fall.
Don't give me a hassle, I am the Rook, the castle.
I am the King, better than ye.
The one who has the power of slave or free,

Who can make any man bow down on his knee.
I am the Bishop, greedy and cunning.
I keep the King moving.
I keep the King running.
I am the Queen who persuades the King
To do my whim, what I say or sing.
I can order the Pawn to the front of a fight.
With a wave of my hand, I can kill the Knight.
Goodbye Bishop, you've lost your position.
The Castle is now out of commission.

STEPPING STONES

Writers want their words to live on long after they're gone. One way to do that is to write them down in cement. Stepping stones look great in the garden, and they'll inspire visitors for years to come.

WHAT YOU NEED

- ✎ Reusable plastic stepping stone mold*
- ✎ Ceramic tiles, marbles, glass beads, etc.
- ✎ Plastic insects or other decorative items
- ✎ Your short poem
- ✎ Paper and pencil
- ✎ Scissors
- ✎ Newspaper
- ✎ 2 buckets
- ✎ Water
- ✎ Markers
- ✎ Rubber gloves
- ✎ Dust mask
- ✎ Mortar mix (approximately 8 lb [3.6 kg] per stone)
- ✎ Measuring cup
- ✎ Thick stick
- ✎ Paper towels
- ✎ Craft wire
- ✎ Paintbrush or stick
  *Available at craft stores

WHAT YOU DO

1. These instructions are for making one stone at a time. If you have more than one mold, you can do a few at the same time. Find a level place outside where you can pour and decorate your stones.

2. Plan your design by laying out your decorative items in the empty mold. Set the pieces aside. Cut out paper circles the same size as the mold, and plan how you'll write out the poem.

3. Lay newspaper down where you're going to pour the cement. Fill the mold with water, then pour the water into one of the buckets. With a marker, mark on the outside of the bucket where the water line is. This will tell you how much cement you need for one mold. Dump the water.

4. Dry mortar mix (cement) is dusty and can be irritating to your eyes, nose, and skin. Consider using rubber gloves and a dust mask. Avoid breathing dust when mixing cement. Pour the

64

cement into the bucket until it comes about halfway to the mark on the outside of the bucket. Fill the second bucket with water for washing your hands.

5. Pour 1½ cups (.36 L) of water into the bucket, and slowly add some cement. Stir with the stick, and add water and cement until you reach slightly above the marked line on the bucket. Don't let the cement get soupy. In other words, add water sparingly. It's always easier to add more water than it is to remove it. When you're done mixing, all the cement should be wet and thick like brownie mix or wet sand at the beach.

6. Scrape the sides and bottom of the bucket to make sure all the cement is wet, and there aren't any lumps.

7. Take a handful of cement and pat it down into the mold. If the mixture is too wet, add more

cement until you can't really pour it. Make sure the cement is flat and all the way out to the edges of the mold.

8. Once the cement's filled to the top edge of the mold, gently shake the mold to allow air bubbles to work their way out. Lay a damp paper towel over the surface to gently smooth it out. Then lift the towel off.

9. Place the tiles in around the edge of the surface about ¼ inch (6 mm) from the edge. Push them in so the cement just covers the sides of the tiles. If the tiles are sinking into the cement, wait until it has hardened a bit and you have to gently push the tiles in. When you've got them all in, gently shake the mold to allow cement to fill in depressions around the tiles.

10. To embed objects like rubber insects in the cement, first wrap craft wire around the body of the object so the wire can act as an anchor. Use markers to make sure

the wire is the same color as the object.

11. Sink the wire anchors into the cement, and gently shake the mold to fill in around the wires. Push the insect or other object down until its feet are resting lightly on the surface. Smooth out rough spots on the surface with a damp paper towel.

12. To write the words, use the handle of the paintbrush or a stick. Using the design you figured out in step 2, hold the writing tool at a 90° angle to the surface, and poke repeatedly into the cement to rough out the layout of the words. Then, with a paper towel in one hand and the writing tool in the other, carefully dig out cement from the letters and wipe the bits of cement onto the towel as you go along. Otherwise you'll end up with

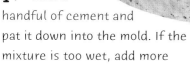

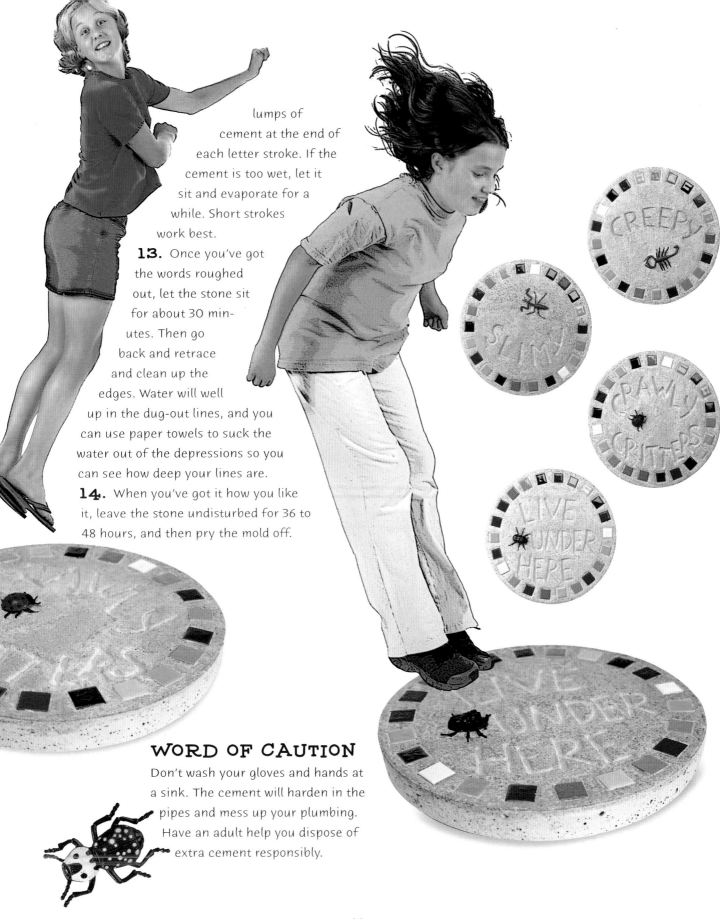

lumps of cement at the end of each letter stroke. If the cement is too wet, let it sit and evaporate for a while. Short strokes work best.

13. Once you've got the words roughed out, let the stone sit for about 30 minutes. Then go back and retrace and clean up the edges. Water will well up in the dug-out lines, and you can use paper towels to suck the water out of the depressions so you can see how deep your lines are.

14. When you've got it how you like it, leave the stone undisturbed for 36 to 48 hours, and then pry the mold off.

WORD OF CAUTION

Don't wash your gloves and hands at a sink. The cement will harden in the pipes and mess up your plumbing. Have an adult help you dispose of extra cement responsibly.

Can't Find a Word to Rhyme with "Purple"? Make One Up.*

Did you know that Dr. Seuss invented the word "nerd"? It first appeared in his book, **If I Ran the Zoo.**

Did you know that if it wasn't for William Shakespeare, your parents wouldn't be able to tell you to take your elbows off the table? In fact, not only did good ol' Bill invent the word "elbow," but he also came up with over 1,700 words, including "zany" and "buzzer." Follow in the footsteps of these great masters, and when unable to find the perfect word, make it up. Here's one fun way:

Take a piece of one word, and a piece of another word, and put them together for a whole new word with a brand new meaning.

Sneeze + Cough = Snough (Don't you hate when that happens.)

*No word in the English language rhymes with month, orange, silver, and purple.

How do you know when something you're writing is finished?

I know when something is finished when it sounds good or complete. Honestly, I don't always know when it's done. Some things must be left incomplete.
—Rachel Kliewer, age 14

That's one of the most difficult parts of the writing process. I will usually rewrite my piece three or four times before calling it done. It is also very helpful to let peers and parents read it over and give comments. Finally, finishing is a personal decision, but you should only call the piece done when you're 100-percent sure that you could not make it any better than it is right now.
—Chelsea Smith, age 13

How do you find privacy when you want to write?

I sometimes write when I'm alone, but when I'm not, I usually do it at night when my parents are asleep.
—Bryan Levine, age 11

I don't really need privacy because sometimes when people talk I get ideas.
—Dana Tarr, age 11

I tell my mother when I'm writing, and she tells everyone not to bother me.
—Devon Dickerson, age 9

I write at the library, and if I'm bothered I move to a quiet corner.
—Jesse Shackelford, age 9

NEWSPAPER NOTES

Have you always dreamt of roaming the streets with a pad of paper and a nose for news? Well, making your own newspaper is easy. All you need is news and some paper to put it on! When you produce your own newspaper you can do everything yourself, or you can recruit your friends to help.

What you need for a newspaper:

A GOOD NAME

The name should be short, memorable, and communicate what the newspaper is about. Print the name on the front of your paper and at the top of each following page. It's also good to put the publication date there.

NEWS

News stories tell the facts of recent events as accurately as possible, explaining Who, What, When, Where, Why, and How. They are impartial and written in the third person. The trick to writing a good news story is to get all of the relevant information in there while being as concise and brief as possible

(but not boring). Always begin your story with the fact or facts that will captivate your readers. (The who, or the what, or the when, or the where, or the why, or the how, or any combination of these). Using quotes from real people who are involved, and mentioning as many names as possible, makes things interesting...just make sure your quotes are accurate and all the names you use are spelled correctly.

FEATURES

Features are stories with a strong human-interest angle. News and features often go hand-in hand: the news story tells the most attention grabbing facts while the feature story goes in-depth about the effects on a person or community. (Feature stories can also be unrelated to news, in which case they focus on interesting people and events.) Feature stories can run on the front page of a newspaper, but they often run inside.

EDITORIALS

This is the only place in a newspaper where you get to say what you think. You're still writing in a newspaper, so you've got to present all the facts, but this is the one and only place that you can use the word "I". Remember, the goal of an editorial is to persuade someone to see a topic from your perspective. Insulting your reader is a very bad method of persuasion, so always be scrupulously polite.

COMICS

By far, the best section in any paper. There are four different kinds of comics:

Funny comics: This is what comes to mind when one thinks of a comic strip. There are usually four frames that set up the joke and then deliver a punch line.

Serious comics: These are the soap-opera comics that almost nobody ever reads.

Gag panels: This is a one frame, one-liner. A gag panel usually has a caption rather than a dialogue box.

Political cartoons: Any of the above that deals with political

issues. These usually are a direct commentary, satirical or humorous, on current events. They are found on the editorial page rather than with the rest of the comics.

CLASSIFIED ADS

This is where your readers list things they want to buy, sell, or find. Check out your local newspaper to figure out what kinds of ads are out there.

ANNOUNCEMENTS

These inform readers about local events. Always list the time, day, and place an event is happening, and be very brief.

GENERAL GUIDELINES

✎ Newswriting should be concise. Tell readers the most important things they need to know about a topic—quickly. Before writing, imagine you just said "You'll never guess what happened!" Then write down exactly what you would say to explain what happened. Then, rewrite what you wrote for accuracy, clarity, spelling, and grammar.

✎ Every word of your paper must be copyedited before it's printed. Copyediting is like proofreading—only harder. A good copy editor makes sure everything is not only spelled correctly and is grammatically correct, but also makes sure everything makes sense and is factually correct.

✎ The front page of your newspa-

per should "tease" to the stories inside, so readers can see your paper has a lot more to offer than just what fits on the front page. Use headlines and page numbers like "Neighbors React to Candy Store's Closing, A3," "Soccer Season Begins, C1'" and "New Book Reviews, B2."

✎ Dedicate space on one of your pages to credit everyone who helped make the paper, listing their names beside their titles (Reporter, Editor, Publisher, etc.). This is called the masthead.

✎ Decide if your paper will be free or for sale. It's best to put copies of free newspapers in various public places such as the library and the grocery store. Don't put your free papers anywhere where they can get rained on or blown away by the wind! (You can also deliver free papers.) If your paper is for sale, it makes good business sense to get subscription agreements from readers before publishing. They pay you ahead of time, then you know exactly who to deliver your paper to. You can also give away or sell your paper at a newsstand you set up in front of your house or at a busy corner in your neighborhood.

FAMILY NEWSPAPER

Let your family and friends read all about it with this magnetic newspaper you can update every day.

YOU NEED

- Steel flashing*
- Metal primer
- Paintbrush
- Paint
- Use of a computer and printer (optional)
- Your articles
- Adhesive magnets
- Picture hanging wire (optional)
- Electric drill (optional)

*Available at home improvement stores

WHAT YOU DO

1. Prime the surface of your sheet of metal. After the primer is dry, decorate the border of the paper with the paint.

2. Decide what you're going to call your paper, and play with fonts on the computer until you have a title you like. Print it.

3. Write and print your articles. Collect images, drawings, etc., to go with the articles.

4. Cut small pieces of magnet for the backs of your newspaper pieces. Peel off the adhesive backing and press to the back of each piece of paper.

5. Place the title and articles onto the steel paper. Play with the design until you like the way it looks. If you want, you can drill holes at both ends of the newspaper and hang it up. Change the articles and pictures whenever you like.

START YOUR OWN NEWSLETTER

With the help of a word-processing program, you can create cool newsletters with images, headlines, columns and more. Ask friends to contribute news and ideas. Think of something you're all interested in, and go for it.

WHAT YOU NEED
- Use of a computer with a word-processing program
- Paper
- Digital images (optional)

WHAT YOU DO

1. The most important decision you and your friends will have to make is what will be included in the newsletter. Make a list of ideas and the sorts of articles and pieces you want in the newsletter. Come up with a name for the newsletter and the headings (what will appear in each newsletter).

2. Decide on the font, point size, and format for your title.

3. Create a template for the newsletter by opening a file in the word-processing program (Microsoft Works or Word work well), and save it as "newsletter template." This means that each time you create a newsletter you'll open this file and immediately save it as something else, such as "July Issue."

4. Most word-processing programs include help in creating newsletters and provide formats for you to use. If you can't find the newsletter fuction on the program, use the help function and look for "newsletter wizard." Then you simply follow the instructions for creating the newsletter. If your computer doesn't have a format for newsletters, you can probably go online to the word processor's site and see if they have any available for download. It's usually free.

5. Play with where to put your headings and how to flow your text. If things don't look right, move them around until you're happy.

Here's a list of possible newsletter topics:

BRAINSTORMING

Here's a list of possible newsletter topics:
- Family update
- Neighborhood happenings: recycling efforts, projects
- Creative newsletter including poems, stories, artwork
- Fanzine: stories, poems, articles on a favorite movie, person, novel, or television show
- Favorite hobby or interest: computers, writing, stamp collecting, skateboarding, science, etc.
- Pets: how to care for, play with, and tend to your pets
- Opinions on world events

The Rumbough Road Repo[rt]

Where'd Cujo the Stray Dog Go?
An Investigative Report
by Margaret Faye

Remember Cujo? Two months ago, a straggly, dirty, stray mutt came into our lives. He knocked over our garbage cans, peed on Ms. Hyatt's roses, and even chased poor old Mr. Gersten's cat into traffic. (Luckily little Tilly survived unscathed.) Jenny Ray named the dog Cujo, and it wasn't long before all of us kids pretty much adopted him. Jenny's mom took him to the vet for his shots, and Cujo was even allowed to stay in Jenny's basement. But he really belonged to all of us. He followed us around when we collected money for the Sullivan's after their only car was stolen, and he was quite fond of barking at the school bus as we returned from school each day. Then, suddenly, he was gone. Nobody knew where he had gone. Until now. Turn to page 3 for the rest of this investigative report.

Neighborhood Notes
by Reggie Gilch

- Ms. Hyatt of 47 Rumbough Road needs someone to mow her lawn once a week. You must have your own mower. Knock on her door after 4 p.m. if interested.

- Jenny Ray's treehouse is off-limits for the next two weeks. She's being punished for not letting her little brother play with her. The Crystal Ball Writing Club will meet in Jenny's basement instead.

- Mike Giambi's bike wasn't stolen, as reported in last month's Reporter. His dad put it in the basement and forgot to tell him.

Gossip
by Jenny R[ay]

What a busy mont[h] it's been. As most of you h[ave] already heard, Jon Stewa[rt and] Allison Smith are once a[gain] an item. This on again, o[ff] again, on again, off again, again—you get my drift—r[ela]tionship is back on track a[fter] Jon promised not to call her [any]more. By the way, Allison ac[ed] the literature exam, but only after staying up way past her bedtime.

In other news, yes, I am grounded, and, so, nobody can hang out in the treehouse for two weeks. What a bummer, and it's all my brother's fault. Okay, I was really mean to him, but he deserved it.

Finally, the sad rumor is true. Gita Wolfe is moving back to her native India. We're all going to miss her and her family. The "For Sale" sign is being hammered into the grass as I write this. Who do you think our new neighbors will be? Gita has promised to write her "fond farewell" in next month's Reporter.

PUT ON A PLAY

The biggest difference between writing a play and a story is that in a play you're writing completely in dialogue. If you want your character to sneeze or scratch his head, you write stage directions. See the short play on the following page for how to write your play.

Act I, Scene i:
In the King's chambers.
Enter Chris and Jake, two swordsmen to the king
Chris: I will fight you to the death.
Jake (scratching his head): Why? What did I do?
Chris (angrily): You called me "Elfy."
Jake: But, I thought that was your name.
Chris: Enough with words. En garde! (raising his sword)
Jake: Grunt. Take that! (thrusting his sword at Chris.)
Chris: Ouch. That hurts! (Chris stumbles backwards to center stage)
Jake: Oh yeah! Here's some more for you.
Chris (falling to the ground at center stage): Now, that really hurts. Oh well.
Jake: (positions his sword over the defeated swordsman.)
Take that Elfy!
FINIS

TRIPTYCH COLLAGE

A triptych is a piece of art or writing on three hinged tablets. Triptychs were used in ancient Rome, and today are used to produce fascinating freestanding works of art.

The wind with their swiftness
The rocks with their steepness
The snow with its whiteness
The lightning with its rapid wrath
And the fire with all the strength it hath
Sung in unison.

The stars and the mist danced
In the dim light of the moon.
A light sprinkle of rain showered the ground
And woke the little creatures,
So warm with its hissing, foaming mouth.

WHAT YOU NEED

- Mat board
- Torn paper
- Glue and water
- Paintbrush
- Stamps
- Awl or thin nail
- String
- Beads (optional)

WHAT YOU DO

1. Cut the shapes for the triptych from the mat board.

2. Tear, cut, and glue paper in an overlapping fashion to the mat board with glue that's diluted with water (1 part water/1 part glue). Use a brush to apply the glue, and then place the papers on the background and put more glue mixture over the top.

3. Use stamps and collage items to further decorate the triptych. The stars in this project are rubber stamped, and the feather and dragonfly charm are glued down. The moon is metallic paper cut and glued to the background.

4. Lay the triptych pieces with the inside panels facing up. This is where you want your words. Write, stamp, or glue your words to the triptych pieces.

5. With the awl or nail, poke holes near the top and bottom of each panel where they'll then connect to each other.

6. Thread pieces of string through the matching holes in the panels to connect the panels together. Tie the string pieces, and add beads to the string if you want.

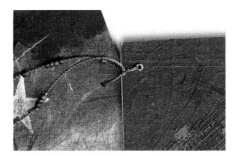

Crimson Sky

Chelsea Smith

As the moon touched the breast of the crimson sky
And the mockingbird began its woes and cries
The winds with their swiftness
The rocks with their steepness
The snow with its whiteness
The lightning with its rapid wrath
And the fire with all the strength it hath
Sang in unison.
The stars and the mist danced
In the dim light of the moon.
A light sprinkle of rain showered the ground
And woke the little creatures,
So warm with its hissing, foaming mouth.

Don't quit your day job

Edgar Allan Poe, author of such masterpieces as "The Raven," "The Masque of the Red Death," "The Tell-Tale Heart," and other creepy, scary stories and poems, spent most of his life broke. That happens sometimes to talented writers and artists. What did poor Edgar do to make ends meet? He wrote jokes and sold them to magazines. How good were they? Here's one, judge for yourself:

Why is a bleeding cat like a question?
Because it's a catty gory.

No wonder he was broke.

HOW COOL HAIKU T-SHIRT

Haiku is an ancient three-line poem that originated in Japan. The first line has five syllables, the second has seven syllables, and the third has five. Though most haiku are about nature, yours can be about anything you want.

WHAT YOU NEED

- Light-colored or white T-shirt
- Use of a washer and dryer
- Use of an iron
- Large sheet of scrap paper
- Colored pencils
- Scissors
- Your haiku or other short poem
- Disappearing blue-ink fabric marker*
- Ruler
- 3-dimensional fabric paint
- Plastic plate
- Flat artist brushes
- Items for stamping (optional)
- Rag (optional)
- Foam brush
  *Available at craft or fabric stores for about the price of a couple of candy bars. There's also a purple disappearing fabric marker that you don't even have to wash out. Your markings will disappear in 24 to 48 hours.

WHAT YOU DO

1. Wash and dry the shirt. Don't use fabric softener. Then, iron it.

2. Sketch out on paper to actual size the design for the T-shirt. If your writing is longer than a haiku, you can go without any graphics,

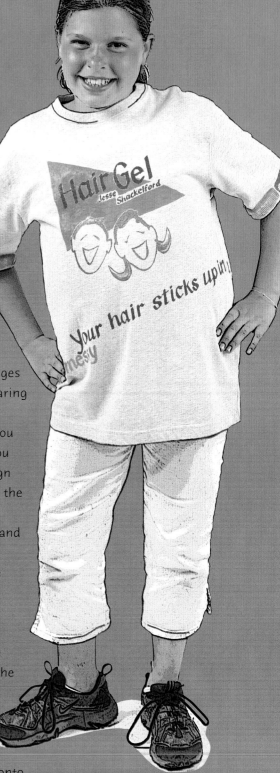

just choose a fun type or handwriting for the words.

3. Cut out the image around the edges of the graphics, and lay it down on the front of the T-shirt.

4. Trace around the outer edges of the design with the disappearing ink fabric marker. You can also draw freehand on the shirt if you wish, or, if the fabric is thin, you may be able to place your design underneath the shirt and trace the design with the marker.

5. Use the disappearing ink and a ruler to draw lines where you want the words to go. Copy the words onto the shirt with the marker. If you make a mistake, ignore it. Just write over it.

6. Paint the design. Read the instructions on the paints for the best results. Don't paint on the back of the shirt until the front is dry.

7. For painting the type, squirt a bit of the fabric paint onto the plastic plate, and use one of the flat brushes to paint onto the shirt.

8. For stamping, use any stamp or object (a small comb was used on this project). Stamps will print best if you fold up the rag and place it under the shirt where you plan on stamping. Dab paint on the stamp with the foam brush, and then print it on the shirt where you want it. See page 15 for more stamping information. Wash the shirt to get rid of the blue ink lines.

Other materials you can use to design your T-shirt: iron-on pencils, fabric crayons, iron-on pens, china markers, and pressure-fax transfer pens.

Hair Gel
Jesse Shackelford

your hair sticks up in
a favorite new cool style,
glossy but messy

On the left sun: *What if your reflection held such power To glance just one day in the next,*

On the right sun: *To see your soul change from blue to brilliant yellow To watch the sun rise and set twice in one day*

ALUMINUM LIT

The aluminum for this project is really easy to work with, and you can cut out any design you want to fit with the writing you've chosen.

WHAT YOU NEED

- 36-gauge aluminum (comes in a roll)*
- Two or three heavy books
- Paper and pencil
- Your writing
- Thin black marker
- Tape
- Ballpoint pen
- Scissors
- Hammer and nail
- Scrap piece of wood
- Jump ring**
- Round-tip pliers
- Leather cord

*Available at craft stores, this aluminum is thicker than foil, yet it's still easy to cut with scissors. Also available in copper.

**Available at craft or bead stores

WHAT YOU DO

1. Flatten out the aluminum under some heavy books.

2. Plan your design, and draw it, with your words, on the scrap pater. This will be your template. Trace over the words with the thin black marker so you can see the words clearly when you turn the paper over.

3. Tape the flattened aluminum onto a smooth surface, and lay the template over the metal with the writing facedown. Tape the template to the aluminum.

4. With the ballpoint pen, trace over the lines of the template and the letters. This will leave an imprint of the template on the aluminum. To create dots, push the tip of the pen straight down and up.

5. Remove the template from the metal, and go back over the words and dots with the pen. Remove the aluminum from the work surface, and cut out the shape with the scissors.

6. Place the project on the block of wood, and tap the nail through about ⅛ inch (3 mm) away from the top edge. This creates the hole for the string.

7. Open up the jump ring with the round-tip pliers, place it in the hole you just created, and close it up.

8. Thread the leather cord through the jump ring, and tie a knot. Gently crinkle the sun rays if you want, while keeping the center oval smooth. If the center gets crinkled or dented, smooth out from the back of the metal by gently rubbing the flat part of your fingernail over the crinkled parts.

Great Reflection

Rachel Kliewer

To possess the power to foretell
Carries deepness
Blackness once said.
To see ahead
Was not meant to be
Await your fate
Your destiny
Put faith in your destiny.
But what if your reflection held such power
To glance just a day in the next,
To see your soul change from blue to brilliant
   yellow
To watch the sun rise and set twice in one day.
To see what comes,
Black or white.
Anticipate,
Worry—just maybe.
Could your body withhold such an almighty gift?
Would you want to see the coming of years?
Could you stand just one day
Or want two days instead?
Greedy, greedy.
For what if a day, you looked in the mirror
Your reflection was no longer there?

CALLING ALL MUSES!

Stuck? Staring at a blank page? Feel like packing it in? Then, it's time to call on your muse. What's a muse? Well, think of the muses as superheroes for writer's block.

In Greek mythology, the Muses were nine sisters whose sole purpose in life was to inspire artists and help them create. They were the daughters of Zeus (head honcho of the gods) and Mnemosyne (the goddess of memory). Each sister specialized in an art or area of study, and she would help humans who wanted to pursue her specialty. In ancient Greece, poets, actors, storytellers, and dancers would start their performances by asking their particular muse to help them do their best work. There were festivals and shrines to the muses, and schools named after them.

Nowadays, people use the word muse to describe anyone or anything that inspires a person's creative urges. Photographers and designers often have a "muse" who they say is the source of all their inspiration. Some people are even inspired by their cats and dogs. Who or what is your muse? Try thinking about that person or pet or thing, and see if it helps your creativity. Or just close your eyes and clear your mind. Maybe one of the muses will pay you a visit:

Terpsichore: dance
Thalia: comedy
Clio: history
Erato: love poetry
Calliope: epic poetry
Euterpe: music
Urania: astronomy
Melpomene: tragedy
Polyhymnia: sacred poetry

Some modern muses perhaps?
Headhurtsalotato: Homework
Spamiopia: E-mail
Thanksomuchope: Thank you notes
Sweetootheroia: Creative snacking

POP-UP BOOK

The pop-ups you design can be any shape, but the size and placement are important to make the piece work. Your pop-ups can be words, images, or both.

I FLY ACROSS THE MOON.

Flying

I fly across the moon. The wolves run like the wind through my hair. The owl's eyes glow like monsters' eyes blinking. I fly with the eagles in the sky.

Wilkin Hanaway

WHAT YOU NEED

- 8½ x 11-inch (21.6 x 27.9 cm) printer paper, in different colors
- Scissors
- Pencil
- Your writing
- Double-stick tape
- Card stock (for cover)

WHAT YOU DO

1. Decide what you want your pop-up to look like. Design your pages and figure out how many you'll need for your book. Use different colors of paper for the different pop-ups. When designing pop-ups, refer to figure 1.

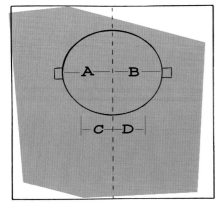

Figure 1

2. Fold the background paper in half lengthwise until you have enough pages for your book. Open up your first spread, and place it on your work space so it looks like a "V" or valley.

3. Cut out the pop-up piece. Experiment until you have created a pop-up that's not so big that it sticks out when the page is folded closed.

4. Find the exact center of the pop-up, and mark it lightly with a pencil. Fold it in half like a mountain.

5. Place the pop-up "mountain" over the background "valley." Determine how much you want it to pop up. Once you've got the positioning just right, mark lightly with the pencil where the middle edges of the pop-up lay on the background. This is where you'll attach the pop-up (your C and D measurements shown in figure 1). They must be less than your A and B measurements.

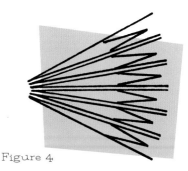

Figure 2

6. Create two tabs with scrap paper. They should be around 1½ inches (3.8 cm) long and wide enough to attach to both the pop-up and the background (figure 2). Fold the tabs in half.

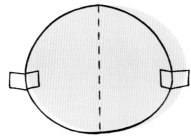

Figure 3

7. Glue the tabs to the middle of the left and right back side of the pop-up. The tab folds have to be parallel with the pop-up's fold, or the page won't close properly.

8. Fold the pop-up so the tabs meet (figure 3). Glue the tabs one at a time, first to your C mark that you made on the background. Then put glue on your other tab, close the right-hand side of the page down on top of the pop-up and glued tab to get the exact placement of the pop-up.

9. Repeat steps 1 through 8 for the rest of the spreads of the book.

10. Fold your spreads and attach them to each other on the edge only with double-stick tape (figure 4).

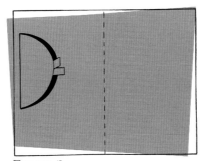

Figure 4

11. Measure the thickness of the spreads when closed (the spine of the book), and take that measurement into account when you're creating the cover. In other words, if your book's spine measures ¼ inch (6 mm) cut a cover that's ¼ inch (6 mm) wider than the paper you used. Fold the cover as shown in figure 5, and attach it to the first and last page of the book with double-stick tape.

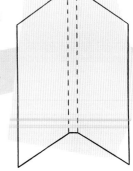

¼"

Figure 5

NUTS AND BOLTS

This cardboard book has a fun binding that uses fabric, some simple sewing, and, of course, a couple of nuts and bolts. Create one for your own work, or team up with some writing buddies for a group book that will showcase all of your writing.

WHAT YOU NEED

- ✎ 6 to 8 pieces of corrugated cardboard, 9 x 13½ inches (22.9 x 34.3 cm)
- ✎ Ruler and pencil
- ✎ Scissors or craft knife
- ✎ Acrylic paints
- ✎ Paintbrush or foam brush
- ✎ Collage items
- ✎ Your writing
- ✎ Glue stick
- ✎ 6 to 8 strips of fabric in different colors, 3½ x 18 inches (8.9 x 45.7 cm)
- ✎ Awl or thin nail
- ✎ Needle and embroidery or crochet thread
- ✎ 2 nuts and bolts with washers

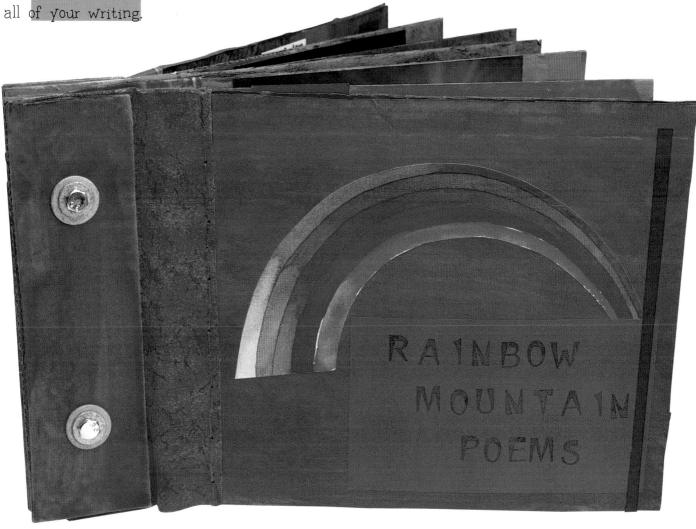

WHAT YOU DO

1. You can make your book any size you want. Simply change the dimensions of the cardboard and fabric. Lay your first piece of cardboard on your work surface, and measure in 2½ inches (6.4 cm). Use the ruler to draw a pencil line at this point.

2. Using the craft knife or scissors, cut the cardboard at the line you just made (figure 1). Repeat with the rest of the cardboard pages. The cardboard strips you just created will be the spine of your book, while the larger pieces are your pages.

3. Paint the cardboard pages with the acrylic paints. Find pictures in magazines that go with your story

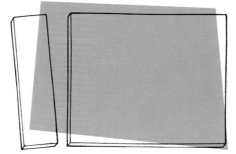

Figure 1

or poem. Use the glue stick to apply the words and illustrations, and other strips of construction paper to fill in open spaces.

4. The fabric strips will be used to reattach the thin pieces of cardboard to the bigger pieces they came from. If you didn't do it this way, you'd never be able to turn your pages or open your book!

5. Place the first cardboard page

along with its strip on your work surface. Choose the fabric strip you want to use to connect the cardboard. Poke holes with the awl or thin nail onto the left-hand edge of the larger piece of cardboard every inch (2.5 cm) (figure 2).

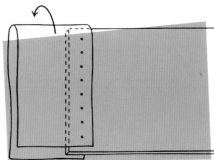

Figure 2

6. Wrap the fabric around the left edge of the cardboard piece (figure 2).

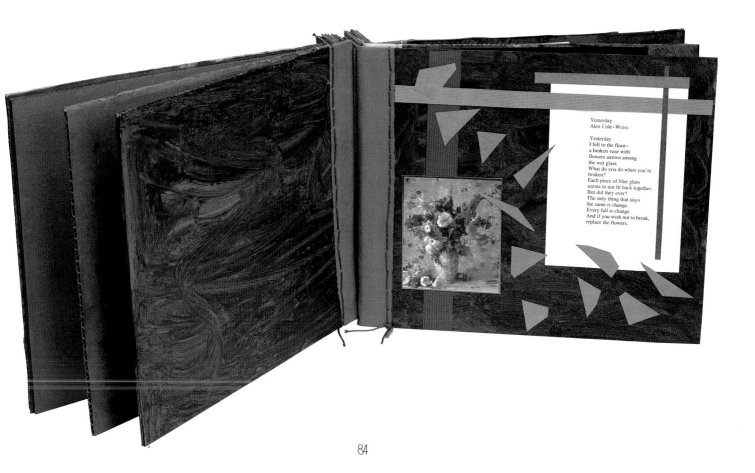

7. Thread the needle, and starting at the bottom of the cardboard page, pass the threaded needle through the fabric and the holes you made in step 5.

8. Work your way up the page until you get to the top (figure 3). Then, turn the page over and work your way down the page. When you get back down to the bottom, tie

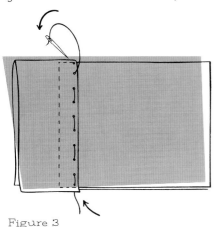

Figure 3

the two strands of thread together (figure 4). Sew the rest of the fabric to the pages of your book.

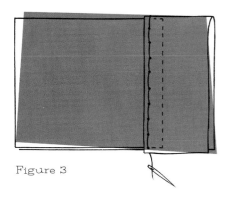

Figure 3

9. Glue the other end of the fabric to the thin piece of cardboard, leaving around ¼ inch (6 mm) of space between the two pieces of cardboard (figure 5). Repeat this

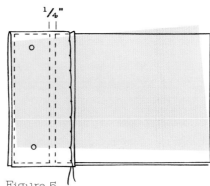

¼"

Figure 5

with the rest of the cardboard until you have all your pages.

10. Poke two holes through all your narrow cardboard strips about an inch (2.5 cm) from the top and bottom. This is where the nuts and bolts will go to hold everything together (figure 6).

11. Stack the book together like a giant sandwich (figure 6). Put one

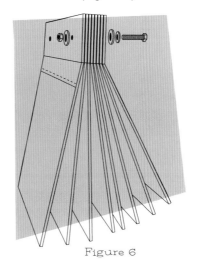

Figure 6

bolt through the top hole in the first page. Now, poke a hole in the fabric with the awl or nail, and place the fabric in. Do the same thing for the bottom hole.

12. Add the next strip and your next fabric until all the pages are connected. Add a nut to each bolt.

Yesterday

Alex Cole-Weiss

Yesterday
I fell to the floor—
a broken vase with
flowers strewn among
the wet glass.
What do you do when you're
broken?
Each piece of blue glass
seems to not fit back
together.
But did they ever?
The only thing that stays
the same is change.
Every fall is change.
And if you wish not to break,
replace the flowers.

It Had to be Said...

Don't be afraid to share your ideas.
—Anna Glodden, age 12

START A WRITER'S GROUP OR WORKSHOP

One of the best ways to get strong, positive feedback for your writing is to start a writer's group/workshop with friends who are also interested in writing. Simply speaking, a writer's group meets once or twice a month to share their thoughts on each other's writing and to offer encouragement, ideas, and advice on becoming more effective writers. In a writing group, everyone gets an equal chance to have their work shared with the group.

WHAT YOU'LL GET OUT OF A WRITER'S GROUP

✏ By reading your writing to others and receiving feedback from them, you'll be better prepared for submitting your work for publication.

✏ You'll have the opportunity to discuss the strong points of your writing, as well as the parts that need work.

✏ You might make some new friends who also like to write.

✏ You get to eat snacks.

HOW TO GET PEOPLE INTERESTED

✏ Post a notice about your new writer's group on the bulletin boards at school or at a local bookstore or community center.

✏ E-mail friends, classmates, cousins, or anyone else around the same age as you that might be interested.

WHAT YOU NEED TO ESTABLISH BEFORE THE FIRST MEETING

✏ When you'll meet. Make sure it is a convenient time for the whole group. Try to meet at least once a month.

✏ Where you'll meet. An empty classroom after school works well (ask a teacher first), or someone's home that has a room with no family traffic during meeting time.

✏ How long each meeting will last. The meeting should be long enough for each member to have a chance to read their work and receive feedback.

✏ How many members to have. If you have more than 5 to 7 members, you may run into trouble reading and commenting on each person's work.

✏ Decide who's going to bring snacks. Snacks are an important part of meeting together. Develop a list of who's going to bring what.

THE FIRST MEETING

✏ Have each member bring one piece of writing they want to read, with enough copies for the rest of the group.

✏ Have the group members pass out their writing, and explain that each member should read them and write comments on them before the next meeting.

✏ It might be a good idea to introduce yourselves to the group, along with what you want your goals to be while in the group, what kind of writing you like, what your favorite books are, etc.

WORKSHOP RULES

✏ At the next meeting, the first reader should read the work, while the others read along silently.

✏ Go around the room and have each member comment on the piece. Have them first start off with something positive about the piece. It's also important that no one in the group makes fun of somebody and/or her writing. Nobody wants to share in an unfriendly environment.

✏ While the comments are going on, the writer should not speak until everyone has commented.

✏ Make sure someone is keeping track of the time so that everyone will have a chance to read and hear comments.

✏ After all comments, each member should hand the marked-up copy of the piece of writing to the reader. Then the next person reads, and you follow the same routine.

✏ After several meetings, you can suggest starting up a newsletter (see page 71) featuring the writing from the group, or even creating a bound book.

QUESTIONS TO ASK YOURSELF WHILE READING SOMEONE'S WORK

✏ What works for you? Why?

✏ What doesn't work for you? Why not?

✏ What parts confuse you?

✏ What sounds interesting to you?

✏ What would you like to read more about?

✏ What supportive comments can you add?

✏ What ideas do you have regarding this piece?

WHAT TO DO WHEN LISTENING TO OTHERS COMMENT ON YOUR WORK

Stay quiet while people talk. If you find yourself saying something like, "Well, what I really meant to say was...," then you probably need to take another look at that section because your reader didn't get it. Don't be bitter. They're not critiquing you as a person, they're trying to help you become a better writer.

ENVELOPE BOOK

For this book, envelopes are your pages, and you can put your words inside. The instructions here are based on the size of envelopes used. By adjusting the measurements for the covers and spine, you can make books for envelopes of any size, larger or smaller.

WHAT YOU NEED

- Card stock (for the spine), 6¼ x 11 inches (15.8 x 27.9 cm)
- Ruler and pencil
- Bone folder or butter knife
- 5 envelopes, 4¾ x 6½ inches (12.1 x 16.5 cm)
- Glue stick or white craft glue
- Stack of books
- 2 pieces of mat board or stiff cardboard for the covers, 5 x 6¾ inches (12.7 x 17.1 cm)
- 2 pieces of decorative paper for the outside covers, 6½ x 8¼ inches (16.5 x 20.9 cm)
- 2 pieces of wrapping paper, for the inside covers, 4¾ x 6½ inches (12.1 x 16.5 cm)
- Scissors

WHAT YOU DO

1. For help with creating the spine, refer to the illustration on page 89. The envelopes will be glued to the card stock that's folded like an accordion. So start out by folding the card stock in half. If you're

The Veil
Hannah Currie

See the way it covers my face.
See the way it restrains my freedom.
See the way it worries the mind.
No education, no rights, no life.
See the cruelty.
See the tyranny.
See the persecution.
See how only our eyes tell you the truth
since our mouths are forbidden to say.
See how we are treated.
See how we are mice in a field of cats.
See how, like an eclipse,
We are not seen
by those who
choose not to watch.
..., see that we are wondrous women,
with hearts like windows
open to the sea,
covered by
the thin veil.

having trouble folding it, lay it on your work surface and score it (see page 19).

2. Unfold the card stock. Beginning at the center crease, measure out ¾ inch (1.9 cm) on each side. Mark these points with the pencil. Measure another ¾ inch (1.9 cm) from those points and mark again. Repeat until you have marked five points on each side of the center crease.

3. Refold the card stock at the center point. Working on one half of the spine at a time, accordion fold the card stock using the points you've measured and marked. Crease each fold well, so that the folds lie as flat as possible, and fold neatly, so that the edges of the card stock stay even as you fold.

4. Arrange the spine on the table so that there are five "mountains"

in the center (see illustration). (If you have it upside down there will be six mountains.)

5. Pretend you're walking from the left to the right side of your spine now. The first "hill" that you get to is the front of mountain one. After cresting the peak, you'd begin walking down the "back" of the mountain, then back up the "front" of mountain two. Working from left to right, apply glue to the "back" side of each mountain, and attach the envelopes. The flaps can face forward or back—whatever you like best.

6. After the envelopes are all glued in place, apply glue to the undersides of each mountain, and then press them together. Place a

stack of books on top of this until the glue is dry.

7. For the covers, apply glue to the back of one piece of cover paper. Center the mat board or stiff cardboard in the center of the paper. Fold the edges of the paper neatly over the sides of the cover. Repeat for the second cover.

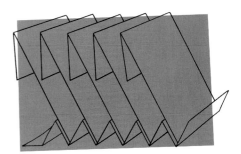

8. To put the book together, refer to the photograph on page 89. Apply glue to the long tails at each end of the book spine. Position the envelopes and spine between the covers. Place the book under the stack of books until the glue is dry.

9. Glue the smaller pieces of wrapping paper inside the front and back covers of the book to hide the tails.

10. Place your poems, stories, or drawings inside the envelopes to complete the book.

It Had to be Said...

Try not to please everyone else with what you write.
—Jenny Spiegel, age 13

The Veil

Hannah Currie

See the way it covers my face.
See the way it restrains my freedom.
See the way it worries the mind.
No education, no rights, no life.
See the cruelty.
See the tyranny.
See the persecution.
See how only our eyes tell you the truth
since our mouths are forbidden to say.
See how we are treated.
See how we are mice in a field of cats.
See how, like an eclipse,
We are not seen
by those who
choose not to watch.
Now, see that we are wondrous women,
with hearts like windows
open to the sea,
covered by
the thin veil.

BRAINSTORMING

If you're suffering from a general lack of writing ideas, or you simply want to experiment, one of the best places to look for inspiration is the daily newspaper. From the obituaries to the police blotter, each section of the newspaper is full of stories, poems, letters, etc. waiting to happen. Write a poem or story about world events. Create fictional life stories of people you read about in articles. Create motives for crimes. Write a poem using only headlines. Tell the story of someone in the news from their point of view. Or simply write a letter to the editor with your take on a local story that sparked your interest. After your family is through with the paper for the day, collect clippings of wild, wacky, weird, fun, and/or interesting articles, and save them in a folder for a time when you're particularly blocked.

SIMPLY A-MAZE-ING

Create six different maze books, each from one piece of paper, to create a sectioned poem, or a series of chapters for a story.

WHAT YOU NEED

- Cigar box
- Ruler
- Calculator
- Square sheets of printer or art paper (size to be determined in step 5)
- Scissors
- Acrylic paints, markers, colored pencils or other decorating materials

WHAT YOU DO

1. Decorate the cigar box to illustrate your writing.

2. In order to determine the size of the paper you'll need to create the maze books, you need to do a little math. Use the calculator to make this easier.

3. First, measure the inside length of the box. Divide by three, and write down the result. For example, nine inches divided by three equals three.

4. Next, measure the width of the box. Divide by two, and write down the result. For example, six inches divided by two equals three.

5. Multiply both your results by four, and you have the size of paper you need for the maze books (3 x 4 = 12; 3 x 4 = 12; so the size of paper you need for this example is 12 x 12 inches). You can find odd-sized paper at craft, office supply, and art supply stores.

6. Fold your first piece of paper in half vertically. Fold it again in the same direction (figures 1 and 2). Open it up and turn it ¼ so it's horizontal (figure 3).

7. Fold it in half. Fold it in half again in same direction (figures 4 and 5). Open up the paper.

8. Figures 6, 7, and 8 show three different ways you can cut the pages for different mazes. The solid lines are cuts you should make, and the dotted lines are the folds you should leave alone. Choose one of the three to start with, and cut your first piece of paper.

9. Fold the boxes of the page back and forth like an accordion.

10. Write your first chapter on this page. Start with a title page, and then write the words down in pencil first. Check to make sure you've got enough room, edit, and then copy over the words and images with colored pencils or markers.

11. Repeat steps 6 through 10 for the next five pieces of paper.

12. Place the maze books in the cigar box.

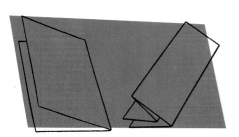

Figure 1   Figure 2

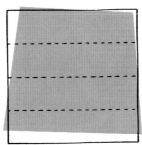

Figure 3

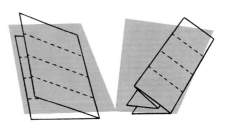

Figure 4   Figure 5

Figure 6   Figure 7   Figure 8

The World Around Us

Jenny Spiegel

Clouds and Rivers
Sky and Moon
Towering Mountains
Calling Loon

Stars and Planets
Grass and Trees
Golden Wheat Fields
Buzzing Bees

Plains and Forest
Streams and Lakes
Gentle Breezes
Hissing Snake

Ferns and Flowers
Sand and Stones
Yellow Sunrise
Cawing Crow

Caves and Caverns
Air and Wind
Purple Sunsets
That's the End

POSTCARD ART

Everyone loves to get mail, but the person you send this giant postcard to will feel extra special indeed. Have fun collecting the materials to make this card, and even more fun mailing it.

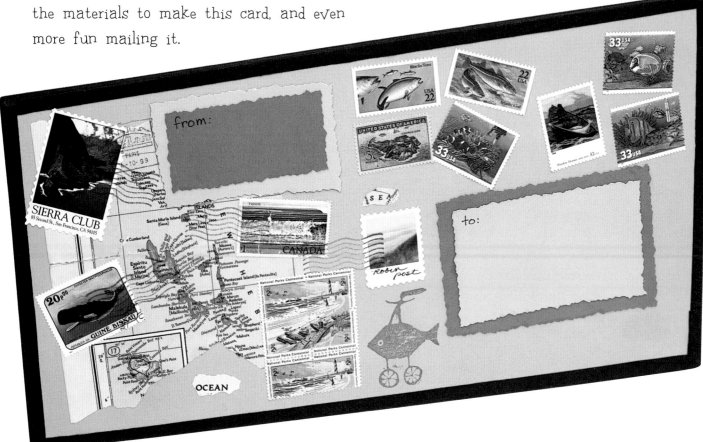

WHAT YOU NEED

- Your writing
- Decorative printer paper
- 2 pieces of mat board, both big enough for your postcard
- Pencil
- Craft knife
- Piece of scrap wood or cutting mat (see page 19)

- Metal ruler
- ¼-inch (6 mm) foam core
- Colored paper
- Tape
- Clear plastic report cover
- Scissors
- Double-sided tape
- Tiny objects or charms less than ¼-inch (6 mm) thick

- Cloth adhesive tape
- Collage items related to your writing
- Craft glue
- Black magic marker (or color to match your cloth tape)

WHAT YOU DO

1. You'll be making a postcard "sandwich"—two layers of mat board with a foam core "filling." The front piece of mat board will be for the address label and the stamps. The back will be used for the poem and windows.

2. Print your poem, story, or other writing. Decorate it if you want.

3. Decide how big you want your postcard to be. Cut one piece of mat board to that size with the craft knife. Make sure both pieces of mat board are color side out, and trace the mat board you just cut onto the second piece. Cut that piece. Label one mat board "front" and the other "back" with a pencil. Use the mat board to trace the postcard onto the foam core, and cut out the foam core shape, as well (figure 1).

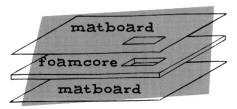

Figure 1

4. Place the "back" piece colored side up on your work surface. Arrange your writing how you want. Cut it in creative ways if you wish. Lightly pencil in an outline of where your writing will be placed, and set the writing aside.

5. To make a window, (see photo detail) first decide where you want it and how big it will be. Lightly trace the window's shape on the mat

board. Make sure the window won't run into the writing, and don't put a window closer than 1 inch (2.5 cm) from the edge of your postcard or another window.

6. Use the craft knife and the metal ruler to cut out the window. Don't try to cut through the mat board in one try—use several firm, steady strokes. If your cuts don't go all the way into the corners, turn the mat board over and recut from the back. Make a second window if you want.

7. Lay the back mat board on top of the foam core, and trace the windows you just cut. Cut out the windows in the foam core.

8. Now take the mat boards and foam core and make the sandwich (see figure 1). Tape a piece of colored paper behind the windows if you don't want white backgrounds.

9. Cut the clear report cover at least ½ inch (1.3 cm) larger than your windows, and tape the plastic down to the inside of the back of the mat board to cover the window openings (figure 2). Make sure the tape doesn't show through the windows.

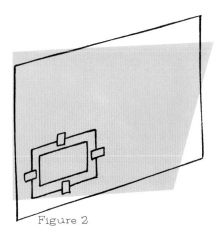

Figure 2

10. Use double-sided tape to tape the foam core to the back of the FRONT piece of mat board. Put long strips of tape down all the way around, almost to the edges of the mat board. If you have some big open spaces, put tape down across it as well.

11. Put little pictures or objects into the window wells of the foam core.

12. Put double-sided tape on the back of the BACK of your postcard sandwich, just like you did in step 10. Press firmly all over the postcard, to make sure the tape holds. If you like, you can cut lengths of cloth adhesive tape and attach them to the outside edges of the postcard. Smooth the edges of the tape down.

13. Glue the writing to the postcard. Decorate the postcard with rubber stamps, canceled postage stamps, collage items, etc. Create address labels, or write the address right on the postcard.

14. Weigh the card to find out how much postage you need to mail it.

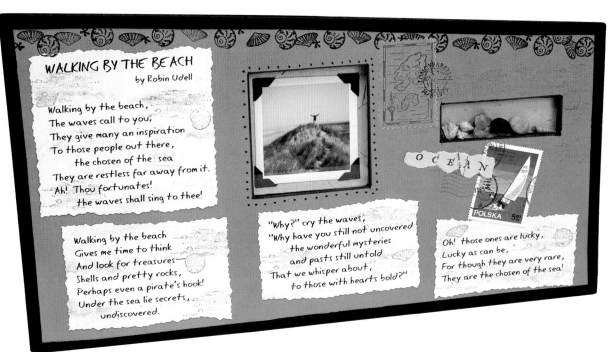

Ask for special stamps at the post office that relate to your theme, or call a stamp dealer (look in the phone directory).

Walking by the Beach

Robin Udell

The waves call to you.
They give many an inspiration to those
   people out there,
   the chosen ones of the sea.
They are restless far away from it....
Ah, thou fortunates!
The waves shall sing to thee!

Walking by the beach gives me time
   to think and look
   for shells, treasures and pretty rocks,
perhaps even a pirate's hook!

Under the sea lie secrets, undiscovered.
"Why?" cry the waves,
   "Have you still not uncovered
   the wonderful mysteries and pasts still untold
that we whisper about to those with hearts
   bold?"

Oh! those ones are lucky,
   lucky as can be.
For though they are very rare,
they are the chosen of the sea.

Strange Mail

Postcard art is sure to catch its recipient's attention, but did you know that the U.S. Postal Service reports that those who want to impress friends, slap mailing labels, stamps, and messages on all sorts of items, including coconuts, pineapples, driftwood, T-shirts, fossils, brooms, stuffed animals, shoes, and even (ready for this) kids. Yes, until the Postal Service forbade the mailing of children, some folks considered mailing a son or daughter a cheap alternative to sending them by horse and buggy. There's even a story that about 100 years ago, a woman put her kid in a box and marked it "Live Baby." How much did it cost to send the kid? About 17¢. What does this have to do with writing?

Absolutely nothing.

PLASTIC POCKET DOORWAY CURTAIN

Create a literary curtain for your room with this fun project. Though there are a lot of steps and materials here, this project is not as difficult as it looks. I promise!

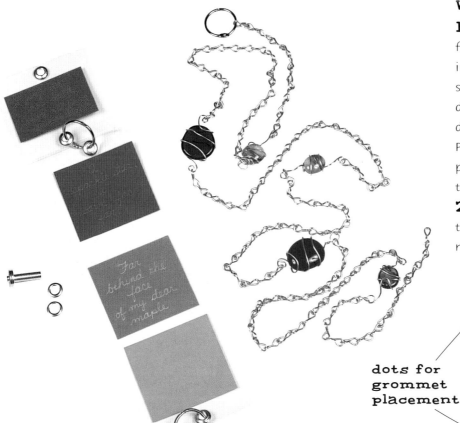

What You Do

1. Measure the doorway from the frame to the floor, and plan on making each strand approximately the same length. Sketch out how you'll divide the poems, and create the different strands of the curtain. Plan on anywhere from 15 to 20 pockets per strand. You don't need to fill up all the pockets with words.

2. With the scissors, carefully cut the negative sheets into different numbers of pockets (figure 1).

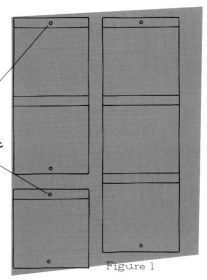

dots for grommet placement

Figure 1

3. Lay out the cut-up sleeves on the floor, and start playing with your curtain design. You can either carefully figure out how each poem will fit in each strand, or you can basically wing it and fill in any empty pockets with photographs, colored paper, etc.

4. Measure the width and height of one of the pockets, and cut out a piece of scrap paper that's the same size.

5. Place a ¼-inch (6 mm) dot in the exact center of the piece of

WHAT YOU NEED

- (supply quantities will vary depending on the size of the curtain you make)
- For the Poetry Strands:
- Tape measure
- 4 to 5 poems, a short story, etc.
- Paper and pencil
- 15 to 20 plastic photograph negative sleeves (6 square pockets per sleeve)*
- Scissors
- Ruler
- Permanent marker
- ¼-inch (6 mm) hole punch**
- Grommet kit**
- 100 (approximately) ¼-inch (6 mm) metal eyelets or grommets (see figure 2 on page 100)**
- Small hammer
- 10 to 13 sheets card stock, various colors

- Pens, markers, and/or gel pens
- 50 (approximately) 1-inch-diameter (2.5 cm) loose-leaf binder rings
- Curtain rod

For the Optional Bead Strands:
- Silver-colored craft wire
- Wire cutters
- Glass stones
- Round-tip pliers
- 26 feet (7.8 m) (approximately) #16 zinc chain (the kind used for hanging signs and plants)***

*Available at photography stores
**Available at crafts stores
***Available at home improvement stores

paper with the marker, and ⅜ inch (1 cm) from the top. You'll use this piece of paper as a guide for punching holes in the pockets.

6. Place the paper guide under the first pocket that will need a grommet, with the dot either on the top or bottom, depending on where the grommet will go (see figure 1). Mark the spot with a small dot from the permanent marker. Use the hole punch to create the hole where the dot is. Repeat with the rest of the pockets. If you keep the strands together on the floor, you'll be able to visualize where the grommets have to go better.

7. Use the grommet kit to set grommets in the bottom holes of the pockets only. Follow the directions on the grommet kit.

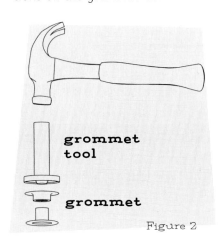

grommet tool

grommet

Figure 2

8. Cut the card stock into rectangles that fit snugly into the pockets, while also leaving room for the grommets. Use the good pen to neatly write out the poems. Put all the poem rectangles into the pockets where you want them. Set the grommets in the pockets' top holes.

9. Put the pocket sections together with the binder rings. Hang the strands from the curtain rod.

Bead Strands (optional) (figure 3)

1. Wrap the glass stones in pieces of craft wire until they're snug and won't fall out. Leave at least 1 inch (2.5 cm) of wire above and below the stones.

2. With the round-tip pliers, create loops on both ends of the craft wire pieces that are holding the stones.

3. Pull a binder ring through one end of the chain, measure about 1 foot (30.5 cm), and use the round-tip pliers to open one of the links and slip the chain apart. Slip one of the wrapped stones into the open link. Open up a second link to connect the chain.

4. Continue doing step 3 until you have a chain the same length as the poetry strands. Make as many chain strands as you want.

Figure 3

ACCORDION FOLDER

If you think it's sort of boring reading a normal book with two covers and pages in between, create this sturdy folder that has a pocket for each chapter of your book.

WHAT YOU NEED

- 2 pieces of mat board or sturdy cardboard for covers, 6 x 6 inches (15.2 x 15.2 cm)
- 2 pieces of decorative paper for the covers, 7 x 7 inches (17.8 x 17.8 cm)
- Ruler and pencil
- Scissors
- Glue
- Stack of books
- Art paper cut to 7½ x 33 inches (19 cm x 83.8 cm)
- Decorative-edge scissors (optional)
- ⅛-inch (3 mm) hole punch or thin nail
- 2 eyelets, ⅛ inch (3 mm), or stapler
- Eyelet setting tool (see figure 2 on page 100)

- Small hammer
- Decorative items
- Your story, printed onto pages measuring 5 x 5 inches (12.7 x 12.7 cm)
- Ribbon, cut to 24 inches (61 cm)
- Large sheets available at art and craft stores

WHAT YOU DO

1. Measure and cut all your paper and boards for this project. For the covers, apply glue to the backs of the decorative paper, and press them into place on the pieces of mat board. Wrap the extra paper neatly and tightly around to the back of each piece of board. Rub any air bubbles away with the flat part of one of your fingernails. Set the covers aside to dry under a stack of books.

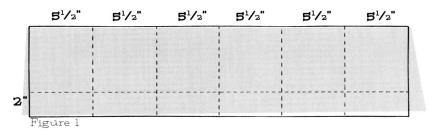

Figure 1

2. Fold the long piece of art paper in half lengthwise. Unfold and lay it flat. Measure out 5½ inches (14 cm) from each side of the center crease and mark. Mea-

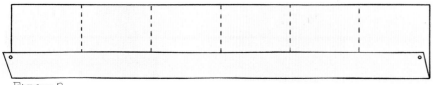

Figure 2

sure 5½ inches (14 cm) from these new points and mark again, dividing the paper into six equal sections (see figure 1).

3. Refold the paper in half at the original crease, then accordion fold the paper at the marks to create six "pages" for the book.

4. Unfold again. Fold up the bottom 2 inches (5.1 cm) of the paper along the entire lower edge to create the pockets (figure 2). Crease it well. If you want, trim along the top of the pockets with decorative-edge scissors.

5. To secure the pockets, punch a hole with the hole punch or thin nail at the top of the folded edge near the front and back edges of the book (see figure 2).

6. Insert an eyelet into one hole. Turn the paper over, insert the setting tool into the back of the eyelet, and tap the top of the setting tool firmly with the hammer to set the eyelet in place. The cone-shaped nose of the tool folds the 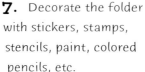 back edge of the eyelet over, trapping it in place and holding the pocket closed. If you don't want to buy eyelets and a setter, use a stapler instead (though it won't look as pretty).

7. Decorate the folder with stickers, stamps, stencils, paint, colored pencils, etc.

8. Refold the folder according to the folds created earlier. Position the back cover of the book in front of you so that the inside is faceup. Place the ribbon across the cover about midway up, so that there's about 6 inches (15.2 cm) extended off to the

right of the cover and about 12 inches (30.5 cm) extended to the left (figure 3). Glue it in place.

9. Cover the back page of the folder (the page that has the BACK of an eyelet showing) with glue, and center it on the inside back cover. Press it firmly in place.

10. Cover the front page (again, with the BACK of an eyelet showing) with glue. Holding the folder closed with one finger, carefully center the front cover over the

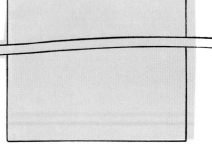

Figure 3

folder and back cover. Sandwich it between the covers, making sure that everything is lined up and the covers match at the edges.

11. Place the folder under a stack of books until dry, then decorate it with stickers if you want. Fill the pockets with your story.

12. To close the book, fold everything together. Bring the long edge of the ribbon across the front of the book to meet the shorter edge, and tie it.

Rachel, Andria, and the Great Journey

(excerpt)
Anna Godden

CHAPTER 1
The Beginning of an Adventure

I was an animal lover, that's all. I wasn't an animal freak, just an animal lover. Well, maybe I was a little obsessed, but I only had 19 pets: let's see...four dogs, Trina, Maya, Kellie, and Brok; six horses, Snowbell, Strider, Strawberry, River, Dewdrop, and Lightfoot; three rabbits, Nutmeg, Clover, and Kitty; two hamsters, Ginger and Spike; three guinea pigs, Blossom, Blue, and Bounce; and a ferret named Flame.

After I had turned 12, my dad gave me the present I had always dreamed about: the chance to go traveling with my friend Andria. I also found out that I was the princess of England, since my mother had been murdered right after I had turned 10. The murderer had been caught, but my mother's life was not saved. But let's skip the details of that, shall we!? So my father had given me the two best things I could have wanted: to be a princess and the freedom to do whatever I liked in terms of exploring the world.

So one day, I didn't want to go to school. I call Andria and she felt the same way. So we decided to go to New York, where the Queen Elizabeth II (QEII) was docked, and I took all my pets with me. Now, since I knew I was the princess of England, I could go on the QEII whenever I pleased. (And I could bring my animals as long as I kept track of them and told them to behave.)

Andria and I called each other "sisters" since we were never seen without each other. We each knew the other's family members and treated them as our own. And they treated us the same way. For instance, when my mom died, Andria's mother took me in and gave me the mother love I had needed at that time. We were all one big family. So, Andria was the second princess of England.

When Andria and I got to the harbor, the crew didn't believe we were the princesses of England. So they called the queen over in England to see if we were

telling the truth. When they found out that we were part of the royal family, they begged our pardon and said we could enter any time we pleased.

When we finally got to our room, we found 20 comfortable beds, each a size that would fit one of my animals. I unsaddled Lightfoot and unpacked Strider and Strawberry. Andria did the same with River, Snowbell, and Dewdrop. We were about to settle in for a nap after our long journey when we received a knock on the door. I got up to answer it. When I opened the door, four greyhounds stood in a neat row outside the door. Two had messages tied to their necks. One with a note and one without stepped up to me; and the other two flew past me to where Andria was sitting. And the suprises were just beginning....

PHOTO TRANSFER BOOK

If you have a lot of photographs to go along with your writing, transfer them to fabric, and create a book you can roll up and put in a pocket.

WHAT YOU NEED

- Paper and pencil
- Your story
- Photographs
- Medium-weight, white cotton fabric*
- Scissors
- Use of a computer with ink-jet printer and scanner
- Photo-altering software (optional)
- Inkjet transfer paper
- Iron
- Paper clips
- Fabric glue
- Needle and thread

* If you go to a fabric store, ask for cotton duck. If not, use white napkins or any nice, smooth cotton fabric.

WHAT YOU DO

1. Make sure you have enough cotton fabric for the book you have in mind. Do a dummy of the book. In other words, a fake book with paper that's the actual size of the book you want, with all the words and sketches of the images so you know what the book will look like. This will also help you deal with the spreads of the book later on.

2. Cut the cotton to the size of one of your spreads. That's two pages side by side. If your book has 10 pages, plus a back and front cover (equaling 12 pages in all), you'll need six pieces of cotton cut to the size of the spreads. You can only print on one side of the cotton, so the pages have to be sewn or glued together after transferring the images.

3. Collect your images, and scan them. If you want, remove unwanted backgrounds and change the images using photo-altering software. Once you've got your images the way you want them, flip them so they're reversed. Check your help menu on the software you're using if you can't figure out how to do this.

4. Fill the paper tray of your printer with inkjet transfer paper. (Follow the instructions on the paper box.) Print each image onto the transfer paper. Trim images to the actual page size of the book, if needed.

5. Iron the cotton fabric (your pages). Place the fabric pages on

One day mom and dad bought a house. Then they decided they wanted a cat too. So they read the newspaper and saw an ad that said, "Cat For Free."

Cat For Free
Handsome, quiet, gray male cat needs a good home. Call 555-1234

So they called the number and we went to get him. He was very happy to have a new family.

top of each other. Fold the sheets in half so you have the shape of your book. Use paper clips to attach two pieces of fabric together. Each clipped pair forms your spreads.

6. Transfer your images, following the instructions on the inkjet paper box. Do one page at a time, and use your fake book as a guide. Add your words with stamps or fabric markers.

7. You can use fabric glue to stick the clipped pages together, or you can sew them or have a parent sew them for you.

8. Sew the book together in the center using the butterfly stitch on page 25.

My Cat
Ashley Price

One day mom and dad bought a house. Then they decided they wanted a cat too. So they read the newspaper and saw an ad that said, "Cat For Free." so they called the number and we went to get him. He was very happy to have a new family. We named our cat Smokey. He is gray. Smokey looks like smoke, so that's why we called him that. He had been abused by the people who had him before, so he was afraid when we brought him home. Smokey climbed into the basement ceiling, and my mom and dad were very scared. They finally got him down and were very relieved. He is still afraid of the doorbell and people who come into the house. Smokey is very lazy. He's 13 years old and a little chubby too. But he is still the best cat I ever had—the best cat in the world.

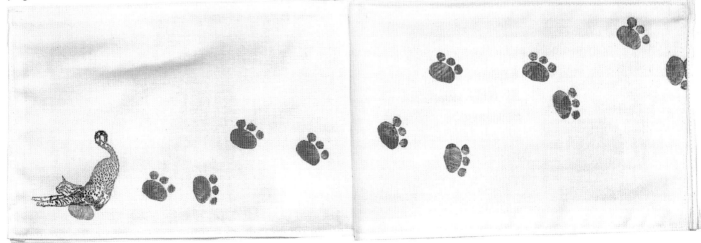

Getting Published

You wrote. You wrote some more. You read, worried, revised, grumbled, polished, and proofread. And just when you thought you couldn't possibly look at

Certificate of Accomplishment

WRITER!

It's Official.

that story, essay, poem, or article any longer, you not only realized you're done, but that it was fun. Yes, it's official, you're a writer. And that piece of writing in your hands looks great, if you do say so yourself. In fact, you're ready for the world to see your words in print.

How do I get published anyway? Isn't it hard to get published? What if nobody likes my work? Maybe I should wait until I'm older. I mean, I'm just a kid. I don't know if I can deal with the rejection. Maybe it would just be easier if I put my finished writing in a folder and hid under my covers.... STOP!

Take a deep breath. There's something about the words "publishing," "submitting," and "manu-script" that can send even the most confident writer into a panic attack. Here's some good news: you don't have to try to get published if you don't want to. (And don't let anyone tell you differently.) There are lots of ways to go public with your writing, including doing the projects in this book. But, if you're ready to start sending your work to magazines, newspapers, and newsletters, take another deep breath and read on. Questions will be answered, and fears will be put to rest.

THE STARTING LINE

In order to get published, you have to send or submit your writing to someone who's willing to put your writing in their magazine or newspaper and perhaps pay you for it. Sounds like a good deal, eh? What are you sending them? A *manuscript*, which is your writing before it's published. Who do you send it to? An *editor*. She's the person who makes decisions about what writing belongs in the magazine. (Yes, it could be a "he" as well.) Is this editor a monstrous being who can't wait to chew up your manuscript, spit it out, and stamp REJECTED all over it? Probably not. Is this editor a

very busy person who doesn't have time to read manuscripts that are sloppy and totally wrong for her magazine? Most likely. So, before you mail your soda stained, hand-written manuscript on stamp collecting to *Cat Fancy Magazine*, consider the next few pages carefully. This information will not make your writing any better than it is; however, it will improve your chances of getting published by focusing your search for a magazine that's just right for your writing, and by helping you make your writing look its best (like when your parents make you dress up for a party).

WHERE, OH WHERE DO I SEND MY MANUSCRIPT?

Unfortunately, there aren't many publishers interested in book-length manuscripts from young writers. It's not unheard of for a 13-year-old to publish a novel, but it doesn't happen frequently. Therefore, this information relates to sending your manuscripts to periodicals (newspapers, magazines, newsletters, or anything else that publishes on a set schedule).

Before you send out your finished manuscript, you need to know where to send it. You'll have a much better chance of getting published if you know of a periodical that publishes the type of writing you're about to send out. This calls for some research and organization.

There are several ways of finding periodicals that will consider your work:

✆ Check the listings on pages 116 to 121. These periodicals specialize in publishing young writers. You can also check out the listings in *The Young Writer's Guide to Getting Published* by Kathy Henderson or *Writer's Market*.

✆ Many magazines have websites that have information on what they're looking to publish.

✆ Go to the library and check out the magazine racks. Also talk to the reference librarians. They have ways of finding what you're looking for.

✆ Ask a teacher for suggestions.

✆ Read and subscribe to writing magazines such as *Writer's Digest*, *ByLine*, or *The Writer*.

✆ Check out some of the hundreds of websites for writers. Just don't try to check them **all** out.

Narrow your search to a few promising magazines, and then send for the magazines' guidelines, and try to find copies of the magazines to read.

GUIDELINES

Most magazines are very nice and will send you specific information about what they will and will not consider for publication. Save yourself the embarrassment of sending poetry to a magazine that doesn't publish poetry by reading the magazine's *writer's guidelines*. These guidelines will tell you just about

everything you need to know to submit a manuscript to them. If you can't find a magazine's guidelines on their website, mail them a request along with a self-addressed, stamped envelope (see page 111 for more information on SASEs, and turn to page 122 for a real, live writer's guidline from *New Moon* magazine).

What Guidelines Tell You

✆ What the magazine considers for publication

✆ Whether the magazine has themes for each issue

✆ Length of pieces they'll consider

✆ How they want you to send your manuscript

✆ What rights they purchase (see page 112)

✆ Whether or not you can send the same manuscript to other periodicals at the same time. This is called *simultaneous submissions*, and it's usually not a wise thing to do. Sending the same manuscript to more than one magazine at the same time can cause problems if more than one magazine ends up interested in the manuscript. One editor will go away angry to have wasted her time and may remember you (not fondly) the next time you send something to her.

✆ How they pay you: could be money, free copies of the magazine, or both. Don't immediately dismiss a magazine that doesn't pay young writers. These magazines are usually good places to start your reputation as a published writer.

☞ Whether or not they prefer a cover letter with some brief information about yourself (more on page 111)

☞ Whether or not to include photographs that go along with the manuscript, and what kinds of images they'll accept (black and white, color, slides, prints, digital, etc.)

☞ How long it takes for them to respond (don't call them!)

☞ Whether or not to send a self-addressed, stamped envelope, also known as an SASE. If you want your manuscript back, you need to mail it with an empty envelope big enough to fit your manuscript, along with enough postage to mail it. Many publishers will simply throw away manuscripts they reject that don't have an SASE.

☞ Where to send the manuscript

☞ And sometimes, to whom (if not, look at a current issue to see who the editor is)

READ THE MAGAZINE

Now, you can get a magazine's guidelines, follow them to the letter, and still find yourself sending in inappropriate work. You should really try to read at least one copy of the magazine you want to submit to. And don't just read the articles you're interested in; read the magazine cover to cover as though you're one of their writers. Study it. Read the table of contents. Figure out what features appear in every issue. Also, try to figure out what the magazine's general style is: formal, chatty, first-person point of view, third person point of view, etc. The more you know about the magazine, the more likely you'll present something they'll be willing to consider.

EXPAND YOUR SEARCH: GO LOCAL

There are probably many publishing opportunities right under your nose. Check out these possibilities:

☞ Local newspaper
☞ Local alternative newspaper
☞ School literary magazine or year-book
☞ Church bulletin
☞ Neighborhood newsletter
☞ Local organization newsletter
☞ Writer's club magazines
☞ Local literary magazine

SCAMS

Once you start looking into different ways to get published, you may be lured into what sounds like a too-good-to-be-true opportunity. **Publisher Seeks Authors! Manuscripts Wanted!** These advertisements and others seem to be promising your publication without all the hard work. In almost all of these cases, these "publishers" are trying to con you. One of my rules of thumb has always been, if there are exclamation points in the ad, run the other way.

What to Beware Of:

✎ Any publisher that wants you to pay them to read your work (called *reading fees*)

✎ Any publisher that wants you to pay them to publish your work (called *vanity presses*)

✎ Any publisher that publishes your poem but then makes you pay (a lot) for a copy of the book it's in

✎ Any contest with an entry fee

Sometimes it's hard to figure out who's trying to con you, especially since most of these scam publishers use flattery to hook you into spending your money. Use your common sense (and that of a friendly adult), and if a publishing opportunity sounds too good to be true, it is.

AFTER THE RESEARCH

Okay, it's time to make a decision. Who will it be: the prestigious magazine that rarely publishes kids' writing, or the kid friendly 'zine that's open to new writers? That's totally up to you. If you don't mind a few rejection slips in your files, then go with the prestigious mag. If you simply want to see your name in print, go with a smaller publication. Also, if you have more than one finished manuscript, then send those out as well. Keep track of where you're sending your writing. One way to do this is to keep a chart like the one below.

LOOK LIKE A PRO

You've got a finished manuscript and a periodical you're interested in sending it out to. You're familiar with the magazine or newspaper, and you've read and followed its guidelines. Now it's time to dress up the manuscript so that it looks professional. That means neatness, punctuation, spelling, and format count. An editor may not even look at a manuscript that's handwritten, sloppy, or simply *stapled together*. I know, you're probably thinking this doesn't sound fair, but remember, editors are usually pretty busy, and if they see an unprofessional-looking manuscript, they will probably assume they'd be dealing with an

Title	Where submitted	When submitted	When returned	Accepted/ Rejected	Paid	Notes
"Dirty Laundry"	Stone Soup	6/30	8/3	R	---	Told me to send more!
"The Big Scoop"	New Moon	7/13	7/30	A	Free copy	Yes!!

unprofessional writer. Hey, there's nothing wrong with being a young, inexperienced, slightly anxious writer—every writer starts out that way. You just don't want to look like one. Follow the steps below, and you won't.

GENERAL ADVICE

✏ Always type your manuscript. The easiest way to do this is to use a word processor. You don't have to have the most up-to-date computer with all sorts of cool programs. All you need is a computer with some sort of word-processing program in which you can save copies of your work. A good printer is a must, as well. Ink jet printers work fine. Go ahead and use a typewriter if you can find one, but if you have a choice, nothing beats a computer.

✏ Use 20-lb, white bond paper. Don't use colored paper, and don't draw on the pages. Don't get fancy here; it won't impress anyone.

✏ Only type on one side of the page.

✏ Don't staple the manuscript together. Use binder clips or paper clips.

✏ Remember, PROOFREAD your manuscript, and then get somebody you trust to PROOFREAD it for you.

THE MANUSCRIPT

Follow the formats below to prepare the manuscript. Editors want to be impressed with your words, not how cool or different your manuscript looks.

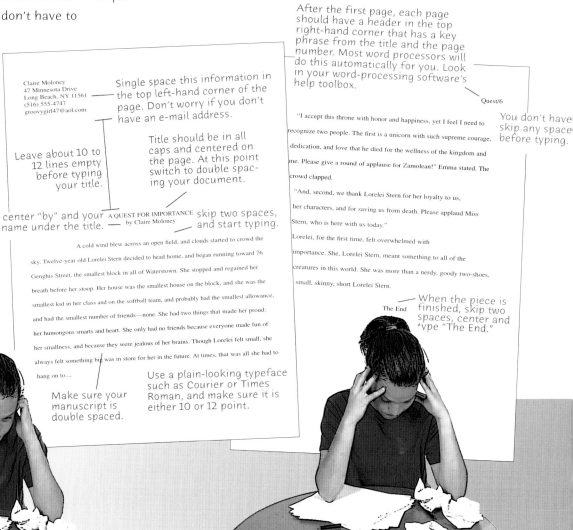

Single space this information in the top left-hand corner of the page. Don't worry if you don't have an e-mail address.

Claire Moloney
47 Minnesota Drive
Long Beach, NY 11561
(516) 555-4747
groovygirl47@aol.com

Leave about 10 to 12 lines empty before typing your title.

Title should be in all caps and centered on the page. At this point switch to double spacing your document.

center "by" and your name under the title.

A QUEST FOR IMPORTANCE
by Claire Moloney

skip two spaces, and start typing.

A cold wind blew across an open field, and clouds started to crowd the sky. Twelve-year old Lorelei Stern decided to head home, and began running toward 76 Genghis Street, the smallest block in all of Waterstown. She stopped and regained her breath before her stoop. Her house was the smallest house on the block, and she was the smallest kid in her class and on the softball team, and probably had the smallest allowance, and had the smallest number of friends—none. She had two things that made her proud: her humongous smarts and heart. She only had no friends because everyone made fun of her smallness, and because they were jealous of her brains. Though Lorelei felt small, she always felt something big was in store for her in the future. At times, that was all she had to hang on to....

Make sure your manuscript is double spaced.

Use a plain-looking typeface such as Courier or Times Roman, and make sure it is either 10 or 12 point.

After the first page, each page should have a header in the top right-hand corner that has a key phrase from the title and the page number. Most word processors will do this automatically for you. Look in your word-processing software's help toolbox.

Quest/6

"I accept this throne with honor and happiness, yet I feel I need to recognize two people. The first is a unicorn with such supreme courage, dedication, and love that he died for the wellness of the kingdom and me. Please give a round of applause for Zamolean!" Emma stated. The crowd clapped.

"And, second, we thank Lorelei Stern for her loyalty to us, her characters, and for saving us from death. Please applaud Miss Stern, who is here with us today."

Lorelei, for the first time, felt overwhelmed with importance. She, Lorelei Stern, meant something to all of the creatures in this world. She was more than a nerdy, goody two-shoes, small, skinny, short Lorelei Stern.

You don't have to skip any space before typing.

The End

When the piece is finished, skip two spaces, center and type "The End."

THE COVER LETTER

A cover letter acts as an introduction to you and the writing you're submitting. It's a good idea to include one unless the periodical's guidelines say not to. The cover letter should not be longer than a page (and a short page at that—you want the editor to read the manuscript, not your cover letter), and should only include:

✏ A short description of the manuscript (a line or two)

✏ A short description of yourself, including any publications or writing awards you've received (though don't be afraid to say you haven't had anything published yet).

Sample Cover Letter

Mildred Mildew
785 Mushroom Lane
Fungus City, WA 74837

April 18, 2004

Bionic Biology Magazine
P.O. Box 9373
Science City, NV 26483-9373

Dear Ms. Biondi,

My name is Mildred Mildew. I have written an essay entitled "Cheez Whiz: Why Every Wombat Should Eat Cheese in a Can." Please consider it for publication in *Bionic Biology Magazine*. It is about the poor diets of the wombats that live in zoos. It explains that contrary to popular opinion, the food that wombats thrive best on is Cheez Whiz. Its purpose is to open people's minds to the fact that all wild animals do not need to eat "natural" food. I hope you enjoy reading it. Thank you.

Sincerely,

Mildred Mildew

Mildred Mildew
785 Mushroom Lane
Fungus City, WA 74837

Manuscript and SASE go in here

Bionic Biology Magazine
P.O. Box 9373
Science City, NV 26483-9373

Bionic Biology Magazine
P.O. Box 9373
Science City, NV 26483-9373

Your SASE

Mildred Mildew
785 Mushroom Lane
Fungus City, WA 74837

Don't confuse your envelopes!

GET IT IN THE MAIL

You need two envelopes, both big enough for your manuscript. One will be your SASE (folded so it fits in the envelope). Make sure you weigh the whole packet and put enough postage to get the manuscript there and back on the envelopes. Go to the post office to weigh it. Before you put the manuscript in the envelope and seal it, make sure you have another copy for yourself. Once it's in the mail, the waiting starts. And the waiting.... And the waiting. Waiting stinks, but there's really nothing you can do about it. Don't call them; however, if you've waited as long as they said it would take, and nothing has happened, do

send them a quick note asking what's going on. And if you still don't hear from them and you want your manuscript back, write to them again, and ask them to send it to you.

ACCEPTANCE (YES!)

It's a great feeling when you get that phone call, e-mail, or letter from a periodical telling you that YES they want to publish your manuscript in an upcoming issue. It's an exciting time, but remember, this doesn't make you a better writer, just as getting a rejection note doesn't make you a lousy writer. It just means that you're soon to be a *published* writer. Congratulations. Some magazines will pay you in free copies of the issue you'll be published in. Others will pay you with money, though don't expect to finance your college tuition with it.

Also, don't be surprised when you finally see your words in print and they don't look exactly the same as the words you sent them. The editor who has accepted your piece may change it around a bit or cut it so that it fits in the space. She might even reword something. In many situations the editor will tell you that she's making the change. If you really don't like what she's doing, tell her. Just don't expect her to change her mind.

KNOW YOUR RIGHTS

As soon as you write something and put your name on it you become the owner of that manuscript (or copyright owner). If an editor agrees to publish that manuscript, that means she's buying the rights to it. There are two different kinds of rights she may ask for:

✏ *First serial rights* or *one-time rights*: After the manuscript is published, you get the rights back after a period of time and can reprint it somewhere else.

✏ *All rights*: The manuscript becomes the magazine's property, and it's no longer yours. You won't be able to publish the manuscript anywhere else. After a period of time you may ask for the rights back, and depending on the magazine, you may or may not be able to get them back.

If a magazine offers to buy all rights, discuss the situation with an adult. Most experienced writers try to avoid selling all rights to a book, but for young writers or any writer just starting out, getting your name in print is more important than being able to reprint a piece.

REJECTION (BOO!)

Even though I wrote about getting accepted for publication first, most likely your first few replies from magazines will be rejection slips. But like I said, this doesn't make you a bad writer. So, why didn't they like it? If you're lucky, the editor will include a quick note telling you, though most likely you'll get a pho-

tocopied form letter rejection that doesn't tell you much. Here are some other reasons why your manuscript could have been rejected:

✏ You didn't do your homework, and the periodical doesn't consider the type of writing you sent.

✏ Your manuscript looked sloppy and unprofessional.

✏ You sent your short story to a magazine that only publishes one short story a year.

✏ You fell in love with your first draft .

✏ The manuscript simply didn't fit what the magazine needed.

✏ The editor didn't like it. (This DOES NOT mean it was poorly written or a bad piece.)

And if your manuscript is returned with a personal note from the editor, that's good news. You got her attention, and it's usually meant as an invitation to try again. So, try again. Try not to let multiple rejections ruin the fun you have writing. The worst thing that can happen is a periodical says "No thanks." Nobody is going to come to your home and unplug your computer and take all your pens away. There are a lot of writers out there, each one trying to do the same thing you are. The ones who eventually succeed are usually the ones who keep trying. Think of each rejection as a learning experience. Keep growing as a writer and learning.

LAST WORDS OF WISDOM

Don't count yourself out just because you're young. Your age can actually come in handy. Editors are often on the lookout for the voice of the next generation (or at least a young writer who can express himself in a clear and interesting way). Hey, maybe you'll even remind an editor of when he was a young writer just like you. Be professional, but also be yourself. Don't change your writing "voice" just to get published. In other words, don't try to write like your teacher, your parents, or any other adult. Be yourself. Enjoy the writing experience, and learn and grow from rejections *and* acceptances. Publishing isn't the everything of writing. It's important, but so is the enjoyment that's to be had by simply expressing yourself with words. Good luck!

EZINES

There are many sites on the World-Wide Web devoted to kid's writing. To find these places, pick your favorite search engine and start looking. (Try keywords like "ezine" and "for kids.") When you find an ezine you like, read it with the same care you would a magazine that you were thinking of submitting your manuscript to. After you've determined that your writing fits, follow the submissions guidelines. Often these guidelines are hidden through links like "help" or "FAQS." If it's not immediately obvious, keep looking. They're somewhere.

Here are some things to keep in mind:

✏ If an opportunity appears to good to be true, it probably is.

✏ Never pay anyone to look at your manuscript.

✏ Never give out your phone number or address over the Internet. If anyone asks you for this information, or other stuff that seems a bit odd, go talk to your parents about it.

CONTESTS

A quick search on the Internet will garner thousands of contests for young writers—many offering money, instant publication, and more. Entering your writing in a contest can be a great way to get published. It could also be a great way to get cheated out of a lot of money. This is another situation where if something sounds too good to be true, it is. Be very careful when entering contests. Many are sponsored by vanity presses (see page 109) or literary agencies that charge "reading fees" or "editing fees." This, however, doesn't mean every contest out there is bogus.

Weeding Out the Fakes

So, how can you figure out if the contest you want to enter is legitimate?

✏ If possible, stick with contests that are run by writing magazines and websites you trust. If you're not sure, ask an adult who knows something about writing, such as your language arts teacher.

✏ Find out who's running the contest you're thinking of entering. If it's a company or organization you've never heard of, do some research, and find out if it's a real contest and not a scam. Most contests advertised in the back pages of writers' magazines are scams.

✏ If the contest is free, you don't have much to lose. If, however, you receive notification that you are a winner, but you need to fork over money to collect your prize...DON'T. You're being scammed.

✏ On the other hand, don't automatically eliminate a contest just because it charges a fee. Many real contests do charge a small fee to cover expenses; however, excessive fees are signs that the contest is a fraud created simply to collect lots of money from you and other unsuspecting writers.

✏ Avoid contests that are run every month.

✐ Read the contest guidelines very carefully. A real contest will provide rules that make sense, including information about deadlines, who's eligible, how to send in your writing, what fees are involved, what are the prizes, how are the prizes awarded, and who's judging the entries.

✐ Who are the judges? A real contest always gives this information. If the judges are published writers or real editors, the contest is more likely to be legitimate.

Entering a Contest

You've done your research, and feel confident you're not about to get scammed. It's time to enter a contest. Here are a few quick tips to make sure your entry gets read and noticed.

✐ Treat each entry as a manuscript you're about to send off to a publisher.

✐ Follow the contest rules exactly as stated. In other words, if the contest calls for entries no longer than 500 words, makes sure you don't send them a story that's 600 words long.

✐ Send for a list of the complete contest rules.

✐ Send in your entry at least a week (or longer) before the deadline.

✐ Keep track of what writing you're sending and where you're sending them. If you haven't heard from a contest after the date they promised they'd notify winners by,

contact them and request a list of the winners. If possible, read the winning entries. (This isn't to torture yourself—it's to figure out what the judges considered the best, and give you a better idea for next time.)

WHILE YOU'RE AT IT....

One way to improve your chances of getting published is to check out lists of periodicals (such as the extensive list provided in the *Writer's Market*), and brainstorm ideas for stories, articles, or opinion pieces for interesting magazines you find.

Or

Think about your interests. If you're into computers or other hobbies or sports, there's probably at least one magazine or website out there on that interest. Become an expert and start writing.

Or

What about that favorite magazine your Aunt Ellen has been renewing for you for five years? You probably know that magazine inside and out by now. Try writing for them, even if you don't particularly like that magazine anymore (don't worry, I won't tell your aunt).

Or

If you have an idea for an article for a specific magazine, you don't have to write the article first. Submit what's called a

query letter to that magazine, asking them if they'd be interested in your idea. The query letter will look a lot like a normal cover letter (try to keep it to one page), except explain the article's premise in detail. Give a good description and outline of what you propose to write. Send it out along with an SASE. And if you've been published before, send along photocopies of one or two of your pieces.

Cool Places to Send Your Writing

NEW MOON: THE MAGAZINE FOR GIRLS AND THEIR DREAMS

Who We Are

Hi! Our names are Ruthie Young and Hillary Boyce. We're on the Girls Editorial Board (GEB) for *New Moon*: *The Magazine for Girls and Their Dreams*. *New Moon* is an international, bi-monthly magazine for girls. The GEB is a group of girls ages 8 to 14 who work together to make the magazine. We get together every other weekend to work on an issue of New Moon. At meetings, we edit and discuss different parts of the magazine. We want to share with you all about what we do on the magazine.

What We Do

First, we meet for a large group discussion. That's where we talk about big topics that need all of our opinions, like local things that we're doing to advertise and spread the word about *New Moon*, upcoming events, and what articles we want to see in the current issue.

Then, we meet in smaller groups, where we edit and discuss the different departments in the magazine. This is where we get specific about our editing. We read all the letters from our readers and

pick which ones will go into the magazine. We also read the feature articles that will be in the magazine and make very specific comments about what we like and don't like about the article, whether it's clearly written, and what the writer still needs to work on.

Finally, we meet in a large group again to do things like look over the laser copy of the magazine, pick cover art, and look over reader surveys. A laser is a proof from our designer that shows what the magazine will look like after it's printed.

What Goes In

When we're picking what goes into the magazine, we look through all the submissions we got for a certain department and try to find a particular article or piece that fits our needs best. Our criteria are different depending on what section we're working on, but one thing that's important to us is that the work we pick for the magazine is done well. We're not looking for perfection, though. We can always edit it—that's our job! We look for something that stands out from the rest of the submissions. For example, out of all the letters we get, we might pick a certain one because it makes a really neat point or shows an opinion that's different from the other letters we get. We might also pick something because we think it'll be inspirational to our readers. And when we're picking feature article ideas for the magazine, we look for ideas that are somewhat out of the ordinary. For our articles about different women from history, for instance, we don't want to cover the same women that everyone hears about in school. Instead, we look for articles on women who've been left out of history books, but who did really cool things that we think our readers should know about.

Another thing that's important to us is that the work in the magazine is done by girls of different ages, usually within our target range (ages 8 to 14). Even though older girls might draw or write better than most younger girls, we're careful to publish things by both younger and older girls because we like to have a good variety of ages represented and because we want to make sure the magazine appeals to girls of all ages.

Our magazine has a different theme for every issue. We pick those themes almost two years in advance! When we're deciding what the magazine themes will be, we consider what kinds of articles will go along with that theme. For example, if we picked a theme that was too specific, like "Foxes," how would we fill up a whole magazine on that subject and still make it interesting? That's why we pick themes that are more general, like '"Friends." One of our themes for 2002 was "Sugar and Spice." We liked that theme because it has two different sides to it. We all know the nursery rhyme "Sugar and spice and everything nice; that's what little girls are made of," and that made us think of stereotypes about girls. But sugar and spice also made us think of cooking, so we were able to cover those two very different ideas in one magazine.

Advice from the Experts

So what can YOU do to improve your chances of getting published?

✏ Find out whether the publication you're interested in submitting to has specific guidelines for how to send in your work. You don't want to ruin your chances of getting in the magazine just because you didn't follow the rules.

✏ Look through at least four past issues of the magazine. That way, you can see what kinds of subjects they normally publish and whether they even accept writing from kids.

✏ Figure out how you can make your writing fit into the style of the magazine. How many words do the articles usually have? What kinds of articles have they published recently? Does the magazine have different themes for every issue?

✏ Proofread your final product very carefully and double-check your facts.

✏ Write a cover letter to the editor explaining what your submission is about and why you're sending it to the magazine.

✏ If your work gets accepted, ask about the publisher's copyright agreement, writer's contract, and payment. At New Moon, our adult managing editors do the contracts with writers and artists (see example on page 124). The agreements say that *New Moon* is buying all rights to the work, how much we're paying for the work, when the deadline for finished work is, and that the writer or artist will get three copies of the issue where their work appears. We pay by the word for written work and a flat fee for art.

✏ If you get rejected from one magazine, DON'T WORRY! It happens all the time! In fact, we have to reject the majority of the submissions we get simply because we don't have a lot of space. It's sad, but true. Keep submitting your piece to other magazines or try doing something different, like changing your idea or revising the article more. Happy submitting!

New Moon®: *The Magazine for Girls and Their Dreams*
P.O. Box 3587
Duluth, MN 55803
www.newmoon.org
1-800-381-4743

BEYOND WORDS

Beyond Words publishes five to 10 children's books each year. A third of their books either feature kids' writing or are written entirely by kids. The kids who submit their writing for contests range in age from seven to 17 years old. (Go to their website for more information.) They also publish fiction and nonfiction written by kids ages nine to 16.

Although their books are not based around themes, they suggest you send them a letter of inquiry to get their writer's guidelines. Word counts vary depending on the specific publication, so make sure to get your writer's guidelines.

After you submit your manuscript, it will take four to six months to learn whether or not they are interested in your submission. They will return your manuscript if you include an SASE with enough postage.

Compensation for publishing your writing is determined on a case-by-case basis.

Contact information:
Children's Division
Beyond Words Publishing, Inc.
20827 NW Cornell Road, Suite 500
Hillsboro, OR 97124-9808
USA
www.beyondword.com

GIRLS' LIFE

Girls' Life publishes six issues per year. They sell more than 500,000 copies of each issue. One or two items in each issue will be written by girls between the ages of 10 and 15. They publish fiction, nonfiction, and poetry.

Although they do not publish theme-based issues, you should read their writer's guidelines on their website. Most pieces range from 200 to 800 words.

After you submit your manuscript, you'll learn whether or not they are interested in it within six weeks. They do not return submissions, so make sure that you make a copy of whatever you send them.

Payment for writing is determined on a case-by-case basis.

Contact information:
Jennifer Park
Assistant Editor
Girls' LIfe
4517 Harford Road
Baltimore, MD 21214
USA
www.girlslife.com

CREATIVE WITH WORDS

Creative With Words publishes 10 to 12 books a year. Seventy-five percent of each publication consists of writing from kids ages five to 19. They publish fiction, nonfiction, and poetry, but they prefer fiction and poetry.

All of their books are theme-based. Send them an SASE for a list of themes and writer's guidelines, or go to their website. Their prose pieces are 800 words, and their poetry is 20 lines (no more than 46 characters per line) or less.

After submitting your manuscript, you will get a reply from two weeks to two months after the deadline for that theme has passed. Include an SASE with your manuscript. They will use this to return rejected manuscripts or to send you notification that your manuscript will be published. They do not return accepted manuscripts, so keep a copy for yourself.

If your work is published, you will get a 20-percent discount on copies of the book you are in.

Contact information:
Creative With Words
P.O. Box 223226
Carmel, CA 93922
USA

HIGHLIGHTS FOR CHILDREN

Highlights for Children publishes a magazine every month. Their magazines are sent to 2.5 million kids, from two-year-olds to 12-year-olds. They publish fiction, nonfiction, and poetry. Approximately 15 percent of each magazine consists of writing from kids.

Although each magazine is not based around a certain theme, they suggest that young writers send them a letter to request guidelines. These guidelines will outline which specific features kids should submit to. Stories should be 200 words or less, and poetry 100 words or less.

After you submit your manuscript, you will be notified when your work is received by the magazine and again if your work is accepted. The time it takes them to make a decision varies depending on which feature you submit for, so be patient. They do not return submissions, so be sure to keep a copy for yourself of anything you send. The magazine does not accept electronic submissions.

Contact information:
Highlights for Children
803 Church Street
Honesdale, PA 18431
USA

INK BLOT

Ink Blot publishes 12 issues of their magazine per year. Approximately 80 percent of each newsletter consists of writing from kids of all ages. They publish fiction, nonfiction, poetry, and black and white artwork.

Although their issues are not theme-based, you should write to them for a copy of their writer's guidelines. Include one U.S. dollar and an SASE with your request, and they will send you a copy of their newsletter with the guidelines. Stories should be 500 words or less, and poetry should be 24 lines or shorter.

After submitting your manuscript, you'll learn within two months whether or not they are interested in it. Include an SASE with enough postage on it if you want to have your manuscript returned.

Authors receive a free copy of the newsletter their piece appears in.

Contact information:
Ink Blot
7547 Pinto Dr. SE
Caledonia, MI 49316
USA

MAJESTIC BOOKS

Majestic Books publishes two to three books a year. These books are anthologies authored entirely by kids ages eight to 18. (The majority of the writing comes from teenagers.) They publish fiction, nonfiction, and poetry.

Although their books are not based around certain themes, you should write to them for a copy of their writer's guidelines before sending in your manuscript. Include an SASE with your inquiry for guidelines so that they'll send them to you! Most of the pieces they publish are 1,000 words or less.

After you submit your manuscript, it takes approximately one to two weeks for a decision to be made about whether or not they are interested in publishing your writing. They will return work they reject if you include an SASE with enough postage on it. You may also electronically file a submission at their website.

Authors will receive a 10 percent royalty on all sales directly related to their inclusion in the anthology.

Contact information:
Majestic Books
Dept. PC
P.O. Box 19097
Johnston, RI 02919
USA
Majesticbk@aol.com

POTLUCK MAGAZINE

Potluck Magazine publishes four issues per year. Almost all of their magazine consists of writing from children ages six through 17. They publish fiction, nonfiction, and poetry.

Potluck
Children's Literary Magazine
THE magazine for the serious young writer ™
Fall 2001 / Vol. 4, No. 4 $5.00 US / $7.50 Can

Creative Corner- Crystal Gayle:
An Intimate Conversation
Poetry * Short Stories * Book Reviews
Fairy Tales * Folk Tales * Fables
Artwork

Although each magazine is not based around a theme, they suggest that you request writer's guidelines. Send an SASE along with your letter of inquiry. You can also find their guidelines on their website. Short stories are usually around 500 words, book reviews are about 200 words, and poetry is 30 lines or less.

After you submit your manuscript, you'll learn whether or not they are interested in it within four weeks. They will return all unused submissions if you include an SASE with enough postage. You can also submit your manuscript electronically through their website.

If your work is published, they will send you a free copy of the magazine in which your work appears.

Contact information:
Potluck Magazine
P.O. Box 546
Deerfield, IL 60015-0546
USA
Susan@potluckmagazine.org
Submissions@potluckmagazine.org

SPRING TIDES

Spring Tides publishes one issue of their magazine per year. Their entire publication consists of children's writing, and their authors are usually ages five through 12. They publish fiction, nonfiction, and poetry.

Although none of their issues are theme-based, you should write to them before submitting anything in order to request their writer's guidelines.

They'll return your submission if you include an SASE with enough postage.

If your piece is published, they will send you a free copy of the magazine.

Contact information:
Spring Tides
The Savanna Country Day School
824 Stillwood Drive
Savannah, GA 31419 USA

SKIPPING STONES

Skipping Stones publishes five issues of their magazine per year. They sell them to schools, libraries, and families. Kids' writing makes up 50 to 70 percent of each magazine. The kids who write for them are from eight to 18 years old. They publish fiction, nonfiction, and poetry.

Some of their issues are theme-based. Send an SASE to them for a list of future themes and writer's guidelines. All pieces should be 750 words or less.

After you submit your writing, they will decide whether or not they are interested in it within three months. Include an SASE with sufficient to get your manuscript back. You can also file your submission through their website.

Contact information:
Skipping Stones
P.O. Box 3939
Eugene, OR 97403 USA
(541) 342-4956
skipping@efn.org
www.efn.org/~skipping

STONE SOUP

Stone Soup publishes six issues of their magazine per year. It's sent to 20,000 people. Everything in the magazine is written by kids between the ages of eight and 13. They publish fiction, poetry, book reviews, illustrations, and anything else written by kids.

Although their issues are not theme-based, but you should write to them for a copy of their writer's guidelines. Include an SASE with your request, or go to their website to look at their guidelines. The pieces they publish are never more than 2,500 words, but there is no minimum word count.

They will not accept manuscripts that are submitted without an SASE with sufficient postage, so be sure to include one! After submitting your manuscript, you'll learn within four weeks whether or not they are interested in it. Authors are paid for their writing.

Contact information:
Ms. Gerry Mandel, Editor
Stone Soup Magazine
PO Box 83
Santa Cruz, CA 95063
USA
1-800-447-4569
www.stonesoup.com

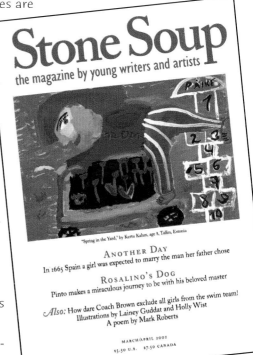

Appendix 1

SAMPLE SUBMISSION GUIDELINES

New Moon is a magazine created by girls for every girl who wants her voice heard and her dreams taken seriously. New Moon is edited by a Girls Editorial Board (girls ages 8 to 14) and they want to hear from YOU!

We fill the following departments with your letters and short creative works.

Dear Luna: The voice of New Moon (letters on any topic under the sun).
How Aggravating: Tell us about how you experience sexism and prejudice.
Howling at the Moon: Tell us about how you and others experience equality.
Ask a Girl: Share problems and solutions with other girls.
Voice Box: Give us your opinions of current controversies.
Check It Out: Write a review of a book, movie, TV show, computer game, magazine, music—especially if not many people have heard of it.
Poetry: Let your muse (or your moose) run free!
The Last Word: Send us your favorite quote by a girl or a woman.

If you've written a longer piece (600–1200 words), submit it as a feature.

Profile: Tell us about great things that girls (like you!) and women are doing today! Please include photos.
Herstory: Write about girls and women of yesterday.
Women's Work: Do you know a woman who has an interesting job? Write about her.
Science Side Effects: Experiment! Send us ideas or articles about science stuff.
Earth to Girls: Eco-conscious girls! Write about all you do for the earth.
Global Village: Girls outside the U.S. write about their lives (write to us for special guidelines).
Girls on the Go: Girl adventurers write about the exciting things they've done.
Fiction: Share your short stories, especially those with strong girl characters and creative subjects that we haven't written about before.

We love to publish your artwork, too!

Luna's Art Gallery: Send us your artwork about anything at all! Use dark ink on unlined paper

Draw Luna: What do you think Luna looks like? Use dark ink on unlined paper.

Luna Tics: Send us teeny-tiny drawings of squiggles and doodles to hide in the magazine.

Cover: If you want your artwork on the cover, send us a self-addressed, stamped envelope (SASE) for special cover art guidelines.

Checklist for Sending Your Stuff In

✔ Choose a department to write for.

✔ Check out our themes to find out what subjects we're going to be talking about in upcoming issues.

✔ Write to your heart's content!

✔ If you're sending your piece by regular mail, make a copy of it first.

✔ Include your first and last names, age, street address, city, state, and zip, and phone number on each submission. We can't consider your letter or article for the magazine if we don't have ALL of this information.

✔ Write your name and the department name on each page you send.

✔ Write the name of the department (like "Dear Luna") on your envelope OR on the subject line of your e-mail message. (We prefer e-mail submissions!)

✔ Keep a copy of your work for yourself, because we can't return it.

We read EVERYTHING you send us, and we send postcards to everyone who writes just to let them know that we got their stuff. Although we can't let you know in advance if we're going to publish your letters or short works, we will let you know if we publish your feature story, poetry, drawing of Luna, or cover art in New Moon—and we'll pay you for it!

Mail your submissions to:

New Moon

P.O. Box 3620

Duluth, MN 55803-3620 USA

Or e-mail us at:

girl@newmoon.org

Appendix 2

SAMPLE CONTRACT

Dear NAME:

As we discussed, we are delighted that you have agreed to provide material for New Moon Publishing, Inc. (NMP) to be published by us in the ISSUE DATE issue of New Moon®: The Magazine for Girls and Their Dreams. This letter, when signed by you, will set forth our agreement with respect to TITLE.

1. You agree that the material will be approximately SIZE and shall be delivered to us no later than DATE. You understand that the material must be satisfactory to us in content and in form. You understand that any revision required by the writer will be completed within 5 workdays after receipt of edited copy.

2. We agree to pay you RATE plus three copies of the issue where your work appears for the material, payable upon publication. You understand and agree the initial license fee covers all uses made by NMP for NMP sponsored publications including electronic transmissions and websites. With respect to fees we receive from others for use of your material, we will also pay you 50 percent of all sums we receive for reprint rights to your material alone, and 50 percent of your initial fee, up to $50, if we use the material in a self-published NMP book, and/or compilations of New Moon material, and/or part of New Moon series published by an outside publisher.

3. You grant to NMP the right to publish your material in NMP magazines, on any NMP website, and in other NMP publications, including books, magazines and compilations in any form, including print and electronic. You also agree that we shall have exclusive reprint rights to your material, provided we pay you as set forth above. You understand that we may edit or adapt the text of your material. You also agree that we and our licensees may use your name, APPROVED likeness and APPROVED biographical data in connection with the promotion of NMP publications.

4. You understand and agree the initial license fee covers use of your photographs, if any, to illustrate the material in the magazine and on any NMP website.

5. You represent and warrant that the material is original and does not violate any proprietary or personal right, either statutory or at common law, of any person, firm or entity or contain anything libelous or obscene, and you shall indemnify and hold us harmless from any claim which if established would constitute a breach of the forgoing warranties. You agree that we may extend your representations and the grant of rights as set forth herein to others, including licensees and sellers of the work.

6. You understand that you are performing the services hereunder as an independent contractor and that no deductions for Federal or State income tax, Social Security or employee benefits of any kind will be made from your payments.

7. You agree that you will not permit the use of this material in any book or other compilation, other than a book written solely by you, without NMP's prior written consent.

8. This agreement contains our entire understanding and may not be modified except in written form signed by both of us. This agreement shall be in all respects construed in accordance with and governed by the laws of the State of Minnesota applicable to contracts made and fully performed therein regardless of its place of execution or performance. You may not assign your obligations under this agreement, but you may assign your right to receive income. A waiver by any party of any breach or default by another shall not be construed as a waiver of any other breach or default.

Please cosign both copies of this letter to indicate your agreement, and return them to me (payment cannot be made until I receive your agreement and W-9 tax form). I will then countersign both copies and return one original to you for your files.

I look forward to working with you.

Sincerely,

Deb Mylin
Managing Editor
New Moon Publishing, Inc.

By: _____   _____
Its: Managing Editor   AUTHOR

_____   _____
Guardian (if needed)   phone number

GLOSSARY

Announcement: A list of upcoming events in a newspaper.

Blurbs: The cool quotes on the back of a book.

Book binding: What keeps all the pages of a book together and in order.

Brainstorming: Thinking of everything relating to your topic, no matter how silly or stupid it seems at the time.

Byline: A sentence or two that tells the reader about the author of the article she just read.

Classified ad: A newspaper listing of things your readers want to buy, sell, or give away.

Cliffhanger: When a chapter ends in the middle of a dramatic situation.

Contract: A legally binding agreement between two parties.

Copyright: The law that guarantees that what you wrote is yours.

Cover letter: The letter that accompanies your manuscript to the publisher.

Editor: A person who helps improve your writing.

Editorial: An opinion piece in a newspaper.

Ezine: An on-line magazine.

Feature: A newspaper story with a strong human-interest angle.

First draft: The initial stage of a manuscript where poor spelling, bad grammar, and weird ideas are welcome.

Glossary: What you're reading right now.

Gutter: The thing on your roof that fills up with sticks, leaves, and dead bugs.

Gutter: The blank space in the middle of a spread.

Haiku: An ancient form of Japanese poetry.

Layout: The arrangement of words (and pictures) on a page.

Manuscript: A piece of writing waiting to be published.

Muse: An inspiring spirit, originally from Greece.

News: The facts about a recent event presented objectively.

Outline: A rough sketch of what's going to happen in your story or book.

Periodical: A fancy name for a newspaper or magazine.

Plagiarism: Stealing other people's words, the worst writing offense EVER.

Proofread: To look over a manuscript and make sure it contains no errors.

Publisher: A company that pays to print and distribute writing.

Reading fees: The charge levied by a publisher or editor for just looking at your manuscript; also a secret code word for "Don't Submit Your Manuscript Here."

Revising: The process of improving your latest draft.

Rights: Things which are granted to you by law.

Scam: A scheme to part you from your money.

Self publishing: Getting your writing read by putting it where people can see it.

Self-addressed stamped envelope (SASE): The envelope with your address on it that you include with every submission you send.

Serial: A story published in installments.

Signature: A stack of pages bound together, and then put into a book.

Simultaneous submissions: Sending the same manuscript to more than one publisher. Usually frowned upon.

Spine: That which fastens the pages of a book together.

Spread: Two facing pages in a book.

Vanity press: A publisher that wants YOU to pay to publish your work.

Writer: You.

Writer's guidelines: Instructions from publishers that tell you exactly what they want and how they want it.

Writer's block: When you get stuck trying to figure how or what to say.

Yes!: Expression of joy to be used upon the successful completion of any step in the writing process.

Zero: The number of mistakes you should have in your final manuscript.

ACKNOWLEDGMENTS

The projects in this book were created by these following big kids at heart:

Karen Timm is a paper, fiber, and book artist who lives in Madison WI. Her passions include using papers from around the world and mixing a variety of fabrics to create 3-D fiber art pieces or artists' books. Her projects are Reading in the Rain on page 61; Calendar of Words on page 36, Photo Transfer Book on page 104; How Cool Haiku T-Shirt on page 76, Pop-Up Book on page 81, Accordion Book on page 39; Scroll Book on page 57; and Simply A-Maze-Ing on page 91.

Leslie Huntley is a totally out-of-work former teacher with a Masters in Education from Wake Forest University. She's also the proud mother of a one-year-old hound dog named Daisy. Her projects are Family Newspaper on page 70; Literary Luminary on page 41; Poetry Lightbox on page 62; Mood Mobile on page 48; and Eat Your Words Place Mat on page 50.

Luann Udell is a nationally exhibited mixed-media artist who lives in Keene, NH. Luann's Postcard Art in on page 94.

Heather Smith combines her experience as an environmental educator with her knack for crafting things to create projects and activities that help kids, their parents, and teachers explore the world. Heather's Magnetic Words appears on page 46.

Karen Page is a mixed media artist who lives in Port Townsend, WA. She began knitting at age 4, and crafting has been an important part of her life ever since. Karen's projects are Nuts and Bolts on page 83 and Triptych Collage on page 74.

Celia Naranjo is an art director for Lark Books. (Hey, she designed this book!) Her Rock & Wire Poetry Holders appear on page 56.

Diana Light is a D. Light-ful (get it!) artist who has this uncanny ability to make everything she touches look absolutely fabulous and instantly cool. Her projects are the Stepping Stones on page 64; Plastic Pocket Doorway Curtain on page 98; Eat Your Words Dinnerware on page 51; Aluminum Lit on page 78; and The Incredible, Shrinkable Charm Bracelet Poem on page 27.

Lynn Krucke is a mixed-media artist in Summerville, SC whose interests include paper arts, beads, fiber, fabric, and polymer clay. Lynn's projects are the Altered Book on page 33; Mini-Book Necklace on page 54; Envelope Book on page 88; Signature Edition Bound Book on page 24; Memory Frame on page 22; and Accordion Folder on page 101.

More Much Needed Thank Yous:

Jane Stanhope and the staff at Rainbow Mountain Children's School in Asheville, NC, for providing some of the most talented young writers I've ever come across.

Nancy Gruver, Deb Mylin, Julie Hoffer, and the staff at *New Moon: The Magazine for Girls and Their Dreams*, for creating the spread on pages 116 to 117, and for letting us use their submission guidelines and contract in the appendix.

Ruthie Young and Hillary Boyce from New Moon's Girls Editorial Board, for writing the New Moon spread on pages 116 to 117.

The wonderful folks at *Beyond Words, Girls' Life, Creative with Words, Highlights for Children, Ink Blot, Majestic Books, Potluck Magazine, Spring Tides, Skipping Stones,* and *Stone Soup,* for sending us all their cool information so we could include it in the book.

The young authors whose writing appears in this book: **Hannah Curie, Wilkin Hanaway, Chelsea Smith, Caitlin Wood, Catrina Frazer, Alex Cole-Weiss, Ty deVries, Anna Godden, Riley Hurst, Jesse Shackelford, Adam Rush, Jenny Spiegel, Dana Tarr, Brianna Huskey, Emily Ellis, K. Lee Evans, Rachel Kliewer, Colleen Ryan, Paul Callahan, Ashley Price,** and **Robin Udell.**

The young authors who submitted work, but, because of lack of room, couldn't be included: **Brianna Thiel, Breanna Weber, Emily Timm, Jessica Lillquist, Emily Moloney, Claire Moloney, Bryan Levine,** and **Devon Dickerson.**

The wonderful, energetic crew of kids who posed for pictures, tested projects, and gave us their best: **Jessamyn Weis, Karla Weis, Wesley Albrecht, Carrie Kubitschek, Christopher "Elfy" Smith, Caitlyn Caskey, Jacob Katz,** and **Nathan Muecke.**

Celia Naranjo, for her collaborative spirit and wonderful design sense.

Rain Newcomb, for researching and writing many of the sidebars and activities, including her awesome work on "Newspaper Notes."

Stacey Budge, for providing much of the information and all of the illustrations for "Design Decisions."

Brian Smith and **Marissa Y. Thompson** for their researching skills.

Joe Rhatigan (hi, dad!) of Long Beach Catholic Regional School (Long Beach, NY) for finding talented young authors.

Shannon Yokeley and **Lorelei Buckley** for their help at the photo shoot, and for assisting with all the production.

Steve Mann for his wonderful photography.

Barbara Zaretsky for nailing down that awesome cover...finally!

Catharine Sutherland for writing "Once Upon a Time" about 100 times.

The usual suspects at Lark Books, including **Delores Gosnell, Deborah Morgenthal, Kathy Holmes, Katherine Aimone, Sunita Patterson, Chris Winebrenner, Veronika Gunter,** and especially **Carol Taylor,** for never losing hope on this one.

Note: The John Ciardi quotation used on page 100 is used with permission from Simmons College. Thanks **Allyson**!

INDEX